These
Strange Ashes

Books by Elisabeth Elliot

A Lamp Unto My Feet

Be Still My Soul

Guided by God's Promises

Journals of Jim Elliot

Joyful Surrender

Keep a Quiet Heart

These Strange Ashes

The Mark of a Man

Passion and Purity

Quest for Love

Path of Loneliness

Path Through Suffering

On Asking God Why

Secure in the Everlasting Arms

Seeking God's Guidance

Shaping of a Christian Family

A Chance to Die: The Life and Legacy of Amy Carmichael

These Strange Ashes

A Deeply Personal Account of
Elisabeth Elliot's First Year as a Missionary

Elisabeth Elliot

Revell
a division of Baker Publishing Group
Grand Rapids, Michigan

© 1998 by Elisabeth Elliot

Published by Revell
a division of Baker Publishing Group
Grand Rapids, Michigan
www.revellbooks.com

Repackaged edition published in 2023
ISBN 978-0-8007-4541-7 (paper)
ISBN 978-0-8007-4546-2 (casebound)

Previously published as *Made for the Journey* by Revell in 2018

Printed in the United States of America

The Library of Congress has cataloged the original edition as follows:
Elliot, Elisabeth.
    These strange ashes : is God still in charge? / Elisabeth Elliot.
      p. cm.
    Originally published: Ann Arbor, Mich. : Servant Publications, c1998.
    ISBN 10: 0-8007-5995-7
    1. Colorado Indians (Ecuador)—Mission. 2. Indians of South America—Missions—Ecuador. I. Title.
    F3722.1.C7E44 2004
    266'.023'092—dc22   2004050944

The image used on the cover shows Elisabeth Elliot in a worship service with Quichua sisters and brothers, eleven days after her husband, Jim, was killed by the Waodani.

Author's note: The names of some of the missionaries in this story have been changed.

For more information on Elisabeth Elliot and her books, please visit her website at www.elisabethelliot.org.

Baker Publishing Group publications use paper produced from sustainable forestry practices and post-consumer waste whenever possible.

23 24 25 26 27 28 29   7 6 5 4 3 2 1

For my sister Ginny
(Virginia Howard deVries)
with love

Contents

Preface

From time to time someone asks me which I think is my best book. I reply that it is a little like asking a mother which of her children she prefers. Each one comes at fairly high cost. One hopes that she has learned something through the production of each, but I doubt that either mothers or authors are the best judges of what they produce. Nevertheless, I confess to feeling a certain tenderness for this book. It tells the story of my earliest lessons in the sovereignty of God—three stunning ones, assigned to me in the first year as a jungle missionary. One of these lessons was solely an act of God. The other two were acts of lawbreakers. In all three, however, God let me hear His clear word: *Trust Me.*

Many times since that year in San Miguel de los Colorados the lesson has had to be repeated. It is not "natural" for me to trust God. It is my natural inclination to worry, to assume burdens never intended for me, to give way to discouragement and even fear. In speaking about God's love and sovereign care over us, I am often asked how we are to accept, as within the context of a loving Father's will, the evil that befalls us because of the sins of others. Is God the author of sin? Did He inspire the murder and theft that tried my faith as a new missionary?

The questions arise again and again, in my contexts, as people tell me of accidents to loved ones, of divorces, handicapped children, abusive husbands, economic disasters, betrayed trust, death. Bad things happen, and so often they happen to "good" people. Shall we assume we are at the mercy of mere chance, or shall we cling to the conviction that God is still omnipotent as well as all-loving? But why did an omnipotent Creator place in His universe creatures with the will to defy Him? Why did He give them in the first place freedom of will, power to choose, when surely He knew that their choices would be evil? Why is the power of causality granted to us, when we make each other suffer in consequence? The power to exercise the will has been delegated. It was delegated to us and God will not usurp it.

Most of the time we like the idea of our own freedom. There are times when we do not at all like the idea of the freedom of others. If we suffer because of their freedom, let us remember that they suffer because of ours. There is something else to remember also: Christ, who willed our freedom, suffered for all of us. Take a long look at what happened at Calvary. The agony there was of the just for the unjust. Why? To bring us to God. Jesus, even in the hands of His captors, was aware that the hour of darkness had its limits, set by His Father. Everything that happened to Him was part of the *appointed way*, yet He said, "Alas for that man by whom he is betrayed." The Son of God, helpless in the hands of wicked humans. What a strange thing. What a mystery Christians proclaim in their faith.

But it's hard to see how that mystery makes much difference when we ourselves are in the pit. Then the why comes from a heart choked with disbelief. We look at the chaos and the destruction. We don't look with much clarity at God. But His attention has not wandered. The Everlasting Arms have not let go their hold.

When Elisha's servant went out early in the morning, he saw a force with horses and chariots surrounding the city.

"Oh master," he said, "which way are we to turn?" Elisha answered, "Do not be afraid, for those who are on our side are more than those on theirs." Elisha then prayed, asking the Lord to open his servant's eyes. The Lord opened his eyes, and the servant saw the hills covered with horses and chariots of fire all around Elisha.

The horses and chariots that the servant had first seen were real enough. He had good reason to fear, if that was all there was. They had no place to turn, it seemed. But for every visible reason for terror, there was an invisible and immensely more powerful reason for trust.

Those fiery horses and chariots are still doing God's bidding. Still the Lord speaks that word to us wherever we are, whatever the forces that oppose us: Trust Me. Never mind the answers to the whys just now—those are Mine. Trust Me.

Over forty years have passed since this story took place. Nearly every time I have told it and tried to explain what

I think God wanted to teach me in it of absolute commit-
ment and trust, someone has asked, "But why did God let
it happen?" Someday they and I will be satisfied with His
answer. Of one thing I am perfectly sure: God's story never
ends with "ashes."

1

The Way In

It is unsettling to me now to know that people who are making a tour of South America can take a short, easy side trip and see the Colorados. They can go in a taxi from the city of Quito to Santo Domingo de los Colorados in a few hours and stay in a nice motel and have a look at a real Colorado Indian any day of the week. The Indians will even dance for you, I am told, or play their wonderful bamboo marimbas. This tells me that everything has changed. I expected things to change, but I did not expect them to change with such frightening speed. The Colorados did not want money twenty years ago. Not money or anything else back then would induce them to come out of hiding on a weekday into the white man's town to do what the white man wanted them to do. Some impression has been made on them, deeply and I am sure irreversibly, and they have been changed.

In the southwest part of North America you can see Indians doing things to amuse white people. There are still those who will "dress up" or dance or demonstrate pottery making or blanket weaving so the tourist will feel that he has been in "real Indian country" and has seen the way Indians live. It has taken a hundred years to bring things to this state. In South America, things have moved much faster. White men, of course, have been there for hundreds of years but had not touched most of the jungle. Indigenous peoples kept on living as they had always lived right on up until the middle of the twentieth century. But then things happened in a moment, in the twinkling of an eye, and they have all been changed. What the tourist pays to see now—is it the Indian I saw?

Dorothy and I, both of us single, both Americans, both students of linguistics, she from Texas, I from New Jersey, rode to Santo Domingo on the tailgate of a pickup. It was no side trip on a vacation tour. Each of us had prayed for years for God's guidance to the place of His choice for our missionary work. We had lived together in a seventeen-dollar-a-month "walkup" in Brooklyn, New York, near a small church group of Puerto Ricans who offered us the free use of the apartment so that we could work with them and learn some Spanish. We were almost the only ones who spoke English in the neighborhood (Bushwick Avenue near what the conductor on the El called "Moitle Avenue"). There was heat in our apartment for a couple of hours a day, and we never knew which hours those would be. There was hot water usually between six and seven in the morning. The Rhinegold Brewery was right next door, and we smelled beer and listened to the noise of trucks all day and all night. There were rats—large black rats, big enough to dump over the garbage pail in the kitchen. It was probably good training for us, living there, and we learned a little Spanish, too. But it proved to be only a smattering, and when we got to Ecuador we spent another six months at it in the capital city of Quito, living in luxury in comparison with our Brooklyn situation, in the home of an educated white Ecuadorian couple who knew no English.

But at last it was time to turn from Spanish studies to the work at which we had been aiming for so long—work with an Indian tribe whose language was yet unwritten. I hoped someday to reduce such a language to writing and translate the Bible. Two English women, untrained in linguistics, needed help in the Colorado tribe. They also badly needed someone to take charge of the school. Here was our chance.

We rode, as I said, on the tailgate of a pickup that belonged to a missionary whom everyone called ET who lived in Santo Domingo. He was a skinny, serious man in his thirties who seemed always to have time to spare, and, unlike most missionaries, never worried about money. He ran some sort of banana business along with his missionary work and spent a lot of time shuttling back and forth between the west jungle and the city. His wife Vera was, fortunately, an easygoing, good-humored woman who did more than her share of the missionary work and, I found out, sometimes went without eggs or some other minor luxury in order to pay off ET's business debts.

ET and Vera picked us up early one morning in September of 1952 for the day's journey down to Santo Domingo. We drove first around backstreets we didn't know existed,

15

ET banging on wooden gates and high walls ("I've got to pick up a letter here"), buying truck parts in tiny alleyways ("I told a guy I'd get these for him"), chatting with slick, disreputable characters in dark banana storerooms. He had contacts. There was no doubt about that. "Señor Eduardo!" a woman called from an upstairs window, and came rushing down to the truck to hand him a packet. "For my sister, please, Señor Eduardo, this little favor!"

We were supposed to "make the first chain." The road to Santo Domingo, ET had explained, was narrow and winding, and twice a day a chain was opened to allow traffic to pass through, going down to the jungle. There was a chain at the other end of the road that was closed to maintain one-way traffic. The "first chain" at our end was at nine o'clock in the morning, but we were still bumping around the cobblestones of Quito at eleven. ET had lived long enough in Ecuador to have learned (perhaps he always knew) how to shrug off the demands of time. Mañana was always good enough. The two o'clock chain would get us to Santo Domingo by midnight or a little before. We did not like any of this, but there was nothing we could do but sit on the tailgate (because the truck was fully loaded with assorted cargo) and go where we were taken.

Shortly after noon, ET finished his rounds. We began the long climb up out of the city, winding around the deep folds of the mountain called Pichincha, where Spanish conquistadores had fought the Incas, higher and higher until we saw the city lying spread out as in a vast bowl below us, velvet slopes on every side, snowcaps gleaming beyond. Quito had seemed to me, when I had first arrived there six months before, an exotic city where the race of time had been slowed nearly to a stop. It was a Spanish colonial city founded in 1534 and retaining still a certain grace from the Old Word—whitewashed adobe houses lined narrow cobbled streets over which jutted carved balconies of lovely dark wood festooned with geraniums. There were delicate wrought iron gates with heavy handmade hinges and door knockers. The green squares and parks had fountains and statuary and some were bordered by graceful colonnades. In six months I had learned to love this city and thought of it as legendary, a city of the faraway and long ago, but as we looked back on it from the high mountain slopes on our way to the jungle, it seemed a last look at the twentieth century. Quito was civilization, and we were leaving it. I was leaving, too, a young man named Jim Elliot, who had studied Spanish with Dorothy and me. We had been acquainted in college, and in Quito he and his colleague, Pete, had lived across the street from Dorothy and me and had eaten two meals a day in the Arias house with us. Jim and I had walked in the pastures on the outskirts of town, had climbed Pichincha and seen the sun rise as the moon was setting over the city, had ridden the bus to the post office on many rainy afternoons, and had explored the byways of the old sections of town, practicing our Spanish on friendly shopkeepers and children. He was heading for the eastern jungle to work with the Quichua Indians, and I knew it would be a long time before I saw him or even heard from him, since we would be separated by the double cordillera of the Andes and communication was exceedingly slow.

The frontier lay before us. "Therefore have I set my face like a flint" were words from Isaiah that had held me steady when I first decided to go to Ecuador, and they held me steady this time as well. Obedience to God was the reason for this journey.

It was a good thing for me to remind myself of the reason because, on top of everything, it was really great fun. It was an adventure and held the thrill of adventure, and if I put my mind on the things set before rather than on the things that were behind, I had no sense whatever of gritting my teeth and doing a thing I disliked. It was the thing I was made for and I was full of gladness.

There were sheep in some of the velvet meadows, and cows, and an occasional horse with an Indian rider. Adobe farmhouses stood here and there in a sheltered hollow or on a hillside by a running brook, screened sometimes by a comb of eucalyptus trees that had been planted to break the tearing Andean winds. Each loop of the cobblestone road brought us higher up the shoulders of Pichincha, and gave us ever vaster views of endless plain and mountain that stretched away north, south, and east. Cayambe was the snowcap to the north, a rounded mass that dominated the famous Otavalo Valley where the Indians live who make wonderful copies of English and Scottish woolens. Antisana, a series of tremendous snowy humps, stood between us and the Amazon basin to the east. To the south towered the near-perfect cone of Cotopaxi, glistening white at the top, spreading out in broad, smooth, black slopes of volcanic ash.

In the village of San Juan, at an altitude of 11,000 feet, we waited for the chain to be opened. ET explained that the cars were counted at the far end, and the number was reported by radio to San Juan.

It was very cold. Heavy drizzle was falling, called the *páramo*, the name also given to the high-grass country where this drizzle is almost constant. Sharp wind was blowing and people from other waiting trucks were standing about, the men wearing wool ponchos pulled tightly about their necks and shoulders, the women covering their noses and mouths with heavy shawls. There was a little shack where we bought ears of hot steamed corn, fried potatoes, and hard-boiled eggs. The corn had huge, soft kernels and was sweet and delicious. We warmed our hands on it as we ate. There were Coca-Colas for sale, some blackened bananas, a mineral water call *Aqua Güitig*, and jars of biscuits and hard candy. A radio was turned to its loudest volume, giving forth the nasal, five-note songs of the Andean Indians, songs sung in Spanish but echoing the loneliness of the bleak mountain country, the lostness of a people stripped and despoiled.

Far down the valley on the western side of the mountains we could see the great cumbersome banana trucks laboring up the steep grade, disappearing into the folds of the ravine, winding into view again, up and up. The sound of the gears reached us faintly. At last they rumbled over the top, coasted down a slight grade into the village, and came to a halt at the chain. Papers were examined, the chain was opened, and they came through and stopped for their corn and eggs and drinks. We waited again. More trucks came. More waiting. The man at the chain decided—we supposed he had counted the reported number of trucks—that the moment had come to let us through. But it turned out that the man was not terribly particular in his count, for we had not gone far down the road when the truck in the front of our caravan came grill-to-grill with another truck on its way up.

"*Caramba*!" shouted the driver.

"*Caramba*!" shouted the other. "Don't you see that I'm on my way down?"

"Don't you see that I'm loaded?" And both drivers got out of their cabs, shouted, thrust clenched fists skyward, raved, and stamped.

There were supposed to be unwritten rules of the road: the loaded truck had the right of way, or the truck going downhill had the right of way. If the truck going downhill met one that was loaded (which was certainly the most common kind of encounter), there was no one to arbitrate and long arguments became the rule. Everyone enjoyed these. They broke the monotony of the journey and gave everybody a chance to look over the crowd in the other vehicle. The drivers and "conductors," boys who usually rode on top of the load and were in charge of collecting fares and seeing to the baggage, loved the opportunity for oratory. Latin courtesies, subtleties, and passions were lavishly demonstrated, the passengers taking part as they felt inspired, and after a suitable interval a decision was reached. The orators leaped into the trucks, engines roared, and off they went again.

I had some idea of counting the horseshoe curves as we traveled. I could see eight or ten below us, but I soon realized the number was deceiving. The journey consisted of nothing but horseshoes, some of them cutting back into ravines much more deeply than appeared from above so that what looked like a single curve turned out to be three or four. The road was treacherous, without guardrails between us and the sheer chasms on one side. On the other side the mountain rose straight up, and at times we bumped across the remains of a landslide that had been mostly cleared from the road. Sometimes a waterfall sprayed our legs or even our heads as we sat on the bouncing tailgate. Once a banana truck coming behind us stopped just under a waterfall. The driver was absorbed in doing something, heedless of the furious shouts from the riders on top who were getting showered with ice water.

Most of the ravines had rivers in them, rushing, clear and joyful, from the heights and plummeting over the rock walls below. There were bridges in some places, but in others the river ran straight across the road and we drove through it. Dorothy and I, having no warning, of course got our feet wet.

The country was wilderness. We saw not more than twenty houses, even though we could see for miles and miles across canyons to the opposite slopes. It was as though we had been dropped into an uninhabited fold of the earth.

The flora changed as we traveled, from alpine meadows to jungle. The forest on the other side of the ravine we were skirting had a draped, stringy, humpy appearance because of the masses of vines and air plants that shrouded the trees. Here and there, there was the burst of a palm or a banana tree, but the general effect was weird and, to me, unearthly, being unlike anything in my own world. It was a journey into a strange dreamland—from the colorful city of Quito, where the gardens were bright with flowers and the white houses dazzled your eyes in the equatorial light, into this deep canyon of grotesqueries, wetness, and increasing gloom. Clouds swirled around us for a time, and then we found ourselves dropping below the clouds into a kind of misty twilight, finally into utter darkness as night fell and not a twinkle of light shone from any house or any star. A curtain had fallen. It was the end of one life. There was no sadness because of that ending, none at all that I remember now. There were both the hesitancy and the expectancy you feel when you have knocked on an unknown door. You do not know who will open it, or what you will see on the other side.

Late in the evening we found ourselves traveling at last over flat land. After all those miles of curves and steep inclines, it was as welcome as the sight of shore to a sailor. We passed through sugar cane and banana plantations. A wooden fence, a saddled and tethered horse, a tiny point of light, told us there must be houses nearby. Then we came to a few shops close by the road, with the din of radios and voices issuing from open doors. Life was being lived here, so far from civilization. People drank and sang in the shops, slept in the silent houses that we could not see behind the banana trees. Of the three foreigners who happened by on the road in the dark, one at least strained her eyes in imagination toward those unseen drinkers and singers and sleepers. "We've come. God has sent us, and we're here now. What will He do for us?"

2

A Missionary House

ET drove the pickup into the yard of his house. Dorothy and I got off the tailgate, rubbed our bruised derrières, and stumbled into the house, helping ET and Vera unload the stuff they had brought. There were wooden boxes nailed and bound with hemp, which Vera called "kerosene boxes," but not because they had kerosene in them now. There were sacks of staples such as flour, lentils, beans, and macaroni. There were enough machine parts to repair every gadget and tool and vehicle west of the Andes, which in fact ET probably intended to do. There were baskets of brightly enameled plates and cups, stainless steel spoons, aluminum kettles of graduated sizes, and there were steel drums of gasoline, sheets of corrugated roofing, and an old battered suitcase. The house was totally dark, but Vera lit two small kerosene lamps—*lamparillas* they are called—and as my eyes became adjusted to the dim light I saw that the house that they called home was a hovel. The missionaries I had known in Quito lived in pleasant, comfortable adobe houses with whitewashed walls and polished wood or tile floors. They had furniture, rugs, and pictures. I expected jungle missionaries to live differently, but not this differently. A grass hut, natural and harmonious and fitting in these surroundings, would not have shocked me. But here was squalor. The house was a sketchy wooden structure, unpainted, and so far as I could tell in the dim light, black. There seemed to be four rooms, each opening into the next, with no hallways or center. Vera told Dorothy and me which was ours, pointed out laughingly that there was no door on it or on any of the other rooms, only curtains for privacy. "Don't mind us, we're just Grand Central Station here!" she said, and for a second I wished I could catch the next train. We found our way to bed.

The next day we had a better look around. The house was indeed black—unpainted wood that had blackened with the dampness and mildew. There were four children who appeared to belong to ET and Vera, though no introductions were made and the children did not seem to speak much English. One or two other people who apparently lived in the house spoke no English. Where they all slept remained a mystery—we had one of the bedrooms, there was a sort of kitchen-living room, and we assumed the other two curtains hid bedrooms. The house was furnished with the barest essentials of tables and chairs or benches of shoddy construction, and Vera cooked on a *fogón*, a sort of sandbox on legs with a fire built on it. Smoke filled the house.

I wanted to get out of this place. The depression it brought me made me feel guilty, for I thought at the time that the ugliness and squalor and lack of privacy were sacrifices appropriate for a servant of the Lord. If I did not like the atmosphere it must mean that I was not yet prepared to lay down my life as I had promised.

The children depressed me. They ought to have spoken to a guest in English, but they spoke hardly at all and always in Spanish. They looked peaked and grubby, they wore no shoes, and their clothes hung on their thin little frames in a most pathetic way. Urchins they were, like their only friends, the town urchins. "Identification" was the idea, I told myself, and it seemed a good principle, but when I saw this demonstration of it in practice something seemed awry.

The yard around the house was practically bald of grass— there were a few tufts in the fence corners, but the rest was slick, hard-packed mud covered with a greenish, scabby crust. There was an outhouse used by the family, a crazy, tall shack emitting a most lethal effluvium, but a steady parade of townspeople were making use of an empty lot next door as a bathroom. They were not seeking privacy, that was obvious, but only space, and judging by the caution with which they stepped, there was little enough of that remaining.

I persuaded Dorothy to go out for a walk. Vera was busy in the kitchen and said she did not need our help. Visitors were coming and going, some of them helping Vera, some of them talking, asking for things, bringing things, the children were in and out, ET was hammering on something. I wanted only to get out of all this for a little while.

We wandered through Santo Domingo de los Colorados. The place looked like a set for a Hollywood western. There was a big, empty square, or *plaza*, mostly of mud, in the center of town, which had a few feeble cannas, a banana tree with shredded leaves, and a scraggly palm trying its best to grow. Wooden buildings faced the square, thatched or roofed with rusted, corrugated iron, the roofs extended to form a covered walkway. The shop doors were wide open, the wares stacked and festooned in the doorways in a jumble of color and tawdriness. The streets were sloughs of deeply rutted mud with standing pools of water. On one side of the *plaza* a row of banana trucks was parked. Men were loading bananas into them from the backs of mules and donkeys and from wooden carts. They were American trucks, I could see from the make of the hoods, but ungainly wooden bodies had been built onto the chassis, and painted bright blue, bright red, pink, yellow, and green, and decorated with pictures, curlicues, mottoes, and names such as "Hitler," "Mother of God," "Little Angel," "The Bull," or "Sacred Heart of Jesus." I came to realize later the huge importance of these trucks. They were the very heart and life of the western jungle. A man might go into terrible debt for many years in order to buy one, and when he had it, he gave himself to it with utter slavish devotion. He named it, first of all, giving it a name of power and protection. This "bull" or "mother of God" would call forth all of his courage and strength and love and would in turn transport and support him, enable and ennoble him, and make him powerful and influential and capable of moving people, of lifting up one and putting down another. There would be no town of Santo Domingo de los Colorados if there were no trucks, and the mayor himself was, like everybody, at the mercy of the truck drivers.

In addition to the pickup we had come down in, ET had a banana truck. It was a big one, painted and named, although I have forgotten what name he gave it—perhaps "The Evangelist." As time went on, it appeared that ET had a great many things going besides his missionary work. In fact, there seemed to be less of the missionary business than met the eye. He had a way of picking up odd jobs here and there, dubious as profit-making pursuits but very profitable, he claimed, as "contacts." A missionary is supposed to make contacts, to get acquainted with people in order to give them his message, and there are many byways. As to the question of legal permission to conduct business on a missionary's visa, ET was not at all bothered. The Lord took care of the details.

Dorothy and I did the whole town in an hour. It was not much of a place. It had little of interest and nothing whatever of beauty. I could not help admitting to myself that I was deeply thankful that God had not appointed me to work here. ET and Vera, apparently, were the appointees, and I was glad of that.

3

A Missionary Journey

From as far back as I can remember, I have been hearing about missionaries. My parents had been missionaries, I was born in a foreign country, and when we returned to the United States, we lived in Philadelphia, close enough to New York to be always meeting boats with missionaries on them and seeing people off for "faraway fields." Missionaries stayed in our home, spoke at our church, and were very much a part of our lives. Betty Scott Stam, who with her husband was beheaded by Chinese Communists, had been one of the guests. Her father, Dr. Charles Ernest Scott, wrote to me when I was a little girl and sent me things from China—a paper fan, some tiger-skin slippers. They were interesting and romantic people. But besides this they were people of high and serious purpose. Their business was to go out and spread the gospel. Spreading the gospel meant missionary journeys like those of St. Paul, related in the book of Acts, when he went out preaching the good news of the resurrection.

Our trip from Quito had been a missionary journey in a sense, but I was glad when ET said he was going out to preach on Sunday afternoon and Dorothy and I could accompany him if we liked. This was to be the real thing. There was a fifteen-mile ride in the pickup over a very rough unpaved road. Dorothy and I rode up front this time, not on the tailgate. We made many stops to let hitchhikers climb on the back. In fact, we stopped for all hitchhikers. ET did not mind how many there were. Where they would find room on the truck was up to them.

We drove through miles and miles of sugar cane and banana plantations before we reached a little hut on stilts, standing in a clearing surrounded by papaya and banana trees. We climbed a notched pole to a veranda made of split bamboo. Eight or ten people were there, apparently expecting us, and from time to time another emerged from an enclosure at the back. We sang some Spanish gospel songs, and ET prayed and taught a lesson from the first chapter of the Gospel of John. "In the beginning was the Word, and the Word was with God, and the Word was God." It was a very familiar passage. I had heard it read at home and in Sunday school and church. I had read it myself in English, and it was the first passage chosen for study in Greek class. The Spanish words, as ET read them, were very simple. But what an ocean's profundity they held! Written nearly two millennia ago, they were being spoken here on this rickety veranda on a warm Sunday evening—spoken as though these people understood them perfectly and accepted the words as well as the Word. They knew (did they?) that there was a beginning to everything. They knew there was, in that beginning, a Word. What Word? Whose Word? Who spoke it? Who heard it? That Word was God.

ET commented and explained in a rather slow, matter-of-fact way, and the people listened soberly. Would they hear? Would the Word—would God—reach them? I was lost in wonderings.

Outraged screams from a pet parrot interrupted the meeting several times, but no one took any notice.

Another rough ride took us to the plantation of an American bachelor who grew bananas, hemp, and citronella grass. I liked his house. It was large and airy, built of bamboo, and lined on ceiling, walls, and floors with woven straw mats. This gave a cool, clean, light atmosphere in perfect contrast with the dim dankness and wretchedness of the missionary house in which we stayed. (But of course this man was here to make money, and had every right to make himself comfortable in the process—so I reasoned.) ET greeted him like an old friend and asked permission to hold a gospel meeting with the plantation workmen. We went to a dormitory—not much more than a thatched roof supported by palm trunks with a makeshift partition between the rooms where the hammocks were slung and the smoky region that served as a kitchen. Through the gloom I could see three "witches"— wizened Indian women bending over glowing embers of charcoal where bubbled a cauldron. We sat down on a plank laid across two boxes in the sleeping part of the house and began to sing. Workmen left their ball game and straggled in, curious. When it was dark, someone brought a lantern and the lantern brought clouds of tiny flies. Again ET prayed and spoke from the Bible. Again I wondered if there were ears to hear. I was glad when the meeting was finished and we could head home in the clear moonlight. There was something oppressive to me about the meeting—was it that I felt that the men did not want to listen but did so only out of curiosity or courtesy or sheer boredom? Or was it failure on the part of the speaker to touch their hearts? Was it perhaps, more sinister—the powers of darkness in a godless place?

There were more hitchhikers. One of them turned out to be a Frenchman who startled us by calling out in the darkness, "Hi, can you give me a lift?" He told us he was homesteading in the jungle. He did not explain why he had come all the way from France. Things seemed rather mixed up. I had come a long way to minister to Indians. In Quito I had seen some at a distance, but I had lived with Spanish-speaking white people. Now, at last in the jungle, I had meant to leave civilization behind. Santo Domingo was a white man's town still, and here, miles from the town, I had come upon an American entrepreneur and a French homesteader. I shifted my horizon a little further. Santo Domingo was just a stopover. When I reached San Miguel de los Colorados, I would begin my work with the Colorado Indians.

At ET's house everything was dark, and there were unidentified bodies stretched out on the floor of the kitchen-living room. The place smelled. It was a mixture of burned grease, onions, smoke, mildew, unwashed people, and the lot next door that served as the town latrine. I climbed into my cot, glad that no one but Dorothy shared this cubicle. The curtain across the door was not much of a barrier, but it gave us some symbolic isolation. I thought of the American's house on the sugar plantation with its light airiness, high on stilts in the midst of the cane like a birdcage, smelling clean and grassy with its lining of straw mats. A great many things determine how people live, and money is not at the top of the list. Choices are always available. What you choose will depend on how you see things: yourself, your work, your right to express taste and desire and personality, your understanding of the love of God as expressed in His creation and order and harmony. "And God saw that it was good." Was it possible that ET and his wife saw their way of living as good? It was possible indeed. Perhaps they really liked it. Perhaps, on the other hand, they chose this way as appropriate to a bondslave of Jesus Christ. They worked in a "dark" place—a place without the light of Christ—and they were willing to live in darkness.

I tried to imagine what our living situation would be when we reached our destination of San Miguel. There were all kinds of possibilities and we would make it good. Tomorrow we would be there.

4

San Miguel de los Colorados

For ninety cents a day you could hire a horse for the ride into San Miguel. Dorothy and I each mounted one of these small creatures that looked to us more like ponies. We were told they were very good at coping with jungle mud, whereas standard-sized horses would never have managed. We stuffed as much as we could into saddlebags, and loaded the rest in kerosene boxes on mules. We rode for three hours through mud. Sometimes the mud nearly reached the horses' bellies and we had mud up to our knees. It was a very wide trail, for each horse kept to the edge, avoiding the worst sloughs as much as possible, and in this way widened it continuously. There was jungle on both sides with only an occasional clearing with a house or plantation. It was beautiful forest, giant trees and ferns and elephant ears crowding each other in unimaginable luxuriance, draped with vines and flowering plants that gave forth unexpectedly sweet scents.

The great breadfruit spread its huge, dark, glossy leaves beside the trail and drooped its heavy brown globes into the mud. Weird and wonderful birds showed themselves to us for brief instances as if to say, "You see, you *are* in the jungle. Here we are." We never saw them again, so we wondered if we had been imagining them. I think I heard the call of a bellbird once.

We met few people—a man following a donkey loaded with *raspadura* (big balls of dark brown sugar wrapped in leaves), a man following a donkey on which a woman was riding, a boy with a couple of loaded mules, several men alone carrying something on their backs. They greeted us and went on their way. A woman called out from one of the houses "*Buenas tardes.*" We did not know it then but these people were expecting us. Word had reached them that two more señoritas were coming, and since they monitored every traveler on the road, they knew we were the señoritas.

In the early afternoon we reached the village of San Miguel de los Colorados. It was nothing more than a large clearing, perhaps two hundred feet in diameter, thickly grown with tall grass and set about with six or eight houses. Two of the houses were enormous barnlike buildings with overhanging thatched roofs. Next to one of them was a neat frame house with a fence in good repair. ET had told us what to look for, and we went to the frame house. As we approached the yard the door burst open and a young woman in a flowered cotton dress came flying out, hailing us with a stream of British English which we could not understand from a distance. This was Doreen Clifford, one of two English women who had

36

been here for several years, trying to evangelize the Colorados. I had met Doreen in Quito and before that in New York when she was "on furlough" and I heard her speak to a group of churchwomen. Her first words in that church meeting, spoken in a high, impassioned tone, were, "Now if any of you ladies go to sleep, I shall *immediately* awaken you with tales of snakes, bats, and sewing up drunken Indians in the middle of the night!" None of them went to sleep. She was about thirty years old, slim, brown-haired, high-spirited, and very earnest.

"Oh, I say!" she cried in her high-pitched voice as she came toward us. "Welcome to San Miguel-on-the-mud!"

We rode through the gate and dismounted, and she took the horses' halters and laid them over a fence post. Another young woman came around the side of the house then, smiling in a rather shy and dreamy way, and we were introduced. This was Barbara Edwards, about twenty-five, of medium height and heavier figure than Doreen, with very wavy brown-blond hair, which she had pulled back as tightly as possible into a bun, but feathery ringlets had escaped the bun and curled around her ears and temples. Both had very fair skin that showed up hundreds of gnat bites on arms and legs. Barbara, too, was wearing a flowered cotton dress that looked as though it had not seen an iron. Both wore tennis shoes, Barbara's white, Doreen's dark brown and snub-toed.

Doreen invited us inside and showed us around. She had a clinic on the first floor. She had taken a course in missionary medicine (mission'ry med'cine, she called it) in London and had cupboards full of bottles and instruments, an examining table and a bona fide dentist's chair. The rest of the first floor was given to dormitory rooms for schoolgirls. It was her dream to have a Colorado school, but until she could start that she had taken in white children who needed a place to board while attending the mission school. She opened a door marked "*privado*" and we went up a flight of wooden steps to her living quarters—a large, pleasant room, screened on three sides, furnished with a few homemade chairs, a folding canvas deck chair, a table or two, a trunk, and a couple of stacks of boxes covered with flowered cretonne. She had curtains and pillows, all of different patterns and colors. In England, she told us, they liked as many patterns as they could get together in one room. It looked a little frantic to me, but it was better than no color at all. A bedroom was partitioned off, containing a real bed with springs that she had brought from England, and another stack of covered boxes that served as a dresser. There was a sort of lean-to kitchen at the back with a *fogón* and several small brass gasoline pressure stoves. A very adequate array of cooking utensils hung on nails above the counter, which was a well-scrubbed board. There was even a little pink plastic sink, also brought from England, in one corner. She had a clothesline that ran from her back door to a pulley attached to a tree so that she could hang up her clothes without going downstairs. It discouraged thieves as well, she explained. I felt reassured in this pleasant house. Doreen had aimed at a modicum of comfort, coziness, and color and my spirits were lifted.

Barbara was still outside. From the window I watched her unsaddling the horses, leading them to pasture, lugging the muddied saddles and bridles into the house. The filmy flowered dress seemed an odd choice for such an occupation, but I soon learned that my own pants and boots were thought very odd indeed. Dresses were the only accepted attire among the women of the clearing.

Barbara had spoken hardly at all, but I recognized that here were two very different women. They dressed alike, they were English, they had wavy hair; there the resemblances ended. They lived in separate houses, and, I would learn, went their separate ways.

When the girl who was working in the kitchen said that lunch was ready, we sat down to a table covered with a green and orange plaid tablecloth. I remember the menu: spinach soup, rice, fried eggs, and tea. There was a pitcher containing cooled boiled milk for our tea, covered with a scalloped crocheted doily weighted around the edges with glass beads. It was a very hot day, but inside the thatch-roofed house it was relatively cool.

It was a strange meal. We were a strange random assortment to have gathered in such a place, but we were drawn together in a unity of purpose. Doreen did most of the talking. She had been in San Miguel the longest, having come from Birmingham, England, when ET and Vera had first settled here. What sort of home she had left in order to do this she did not tell us, or what she had given up or gained in becoming a missionary. We knew only that she had studied medicine and gone on to Bible school and that her heart was here with the Colorado Indians. She told some appalling tales of that first year when she lived in a miserable shack with ET and Vera and their first child. Vera had been pregnant and

ET had been gone most of the time, traveling to Quito to buy supplies for building a decent house, his journeys hampered by rain, avalanches, and illnesses. Doreen herself had almost more "close communion" than she could stand, and it had been quite a year.

But now here we were, drinking tea together over the green and orange tablecloth, discussing the work we would all do. At last, at last, I thought. Under God we would surely do wonders.

Barbara took us to see her house after lunch. It was a big splintery-looking box that stood high on ungainly legs. The walls were of split bamboo, the roof of thatch, very thick and heavy and sodden-looking with greenish moss growing on it. We climbed a flight of steps that were hardly less steep and precarious than a ladder. There was little in the way of furniture—a bed and a few benches and the inevitable *fogón*. Clearly, comfort was not of much importance to Barbara. She laughed and dismissed the house with a wave of her hand.

"I'm afraid you've seen it all now! Not awfully inviting, is it?"

She had not been here as long as Doreen and had not had ET's services as a carpenter and builder, but she appeared quite happy with what she called home. There was an open platform at the top of the stairs that could be called a porch. We stood and looked over the clearing, which was called San Miguel de los Colorados. There were no Colorados anywhere. Of the houses we could see, a few were like Barbara's, a few were without stilts, and there were the two barnlike ones, one of which was to be ours. The Colorados lived back in the forest, Barbara said, miles away. But they rode through here on their way to Santo Domingo. You could say they were within reach.

It is a thrilling thing when you are young to imagine what good things you will be doing in the world and what the world will do to you. It is easy to picture life as pleasant. It is probably even more thrilling if you believe in God and believe that He Himself has called you to do a work for Him in a certain place. San Miguel was the place, I had been called, these women were to be my associates, and the invisible Colorados would soon be visible and work would begin. All was ordered and arranged.

5

A Jungle Home

I sat at a homemade table in the big bamboo and thatched house next door to Doreen's, writing a letter to Jim. I described to him the thick wetness of the jungle drifting in through the wide screened windows, making me feel mildewed and wilted. The paper itself felt limp. A strange doleful whistle carried across the clearing from the edge of the forest, and dozens of birds I could not see twittered in the trees close to the house. I could hear the mumbling of the schoolchildren in the room below my bedroom.

I described the house where Dorothy and I had lived for nearly a week now. There was a long, narrow living room from which opened three bedrooms, all in a row.

Dorothy had the first bedroom. She was in there now, propped up in the big rollaway bed she had brought with her from the States, reading a women's magazine, also from the States. Dorothy was large of heart as well as of body, a comfortable kind of person who had not had the same misgivings I had had about physical comfort. She liked to cook and keep house and did not hesitate to admit it. When we studied Spanish together in Quito she had no clear idea about what she would do as a missionary, but she was sure she would find something. While I had agonized about what the next step would be, she had trusted God, and now here we both were.

The next bedroom was Marta's. She was an Ecuadorian white woman, slim, dark-haired, and dark-eyed. She was only nineteen years old and had just graduated from normal school. Although she came from an upper-class family in Quito, her father had permitted her to venture down into the fearsome forests only because she would be living with two señoritas, a term he was pleased to use for us but that would not, in his mind, apply to jungle people, white or Indian. Marta spoke no English, so we had the great advantage of being forced to speak Spanish at home as well as in our work. It was to be her job to teach the schoolchildren while Dorothy acted as principal.

Mine was the third bedroom, the one nearest the kitchen. Like Dorothy's, it was a corner room with windows on two sides that could not be closed. Screens kept out some of the insects and bats, but there was plenty of space where they could find entrance between the tops of the walls and the thatch. There were cracks, too, in the walls themselves since they were of split bamboo.

There was nothing unnecessary or decorative about anything in the house, since ET had built and furnished it to suit himself, but it was very much more comfortable than their house in Santo Domingo. There were a couple of huge, wooden, slant-seated chairs that might have done rather well on a yacht club deck or a ski lodge balcony, but the scale was overwhelming in a living room. There were some benches, a bookshelf, and two vast tables—one for eating, one for writing.

In the kitchen besides the *fogón* there was a counter made of a board placed across two boxes. Smoke filled the room and seeped along the ridgepole and along the thatch of the rest of the house.

I had been told there were beds available in San Miguel and had left my imported rollaway in storage in Quito. My bed turned out to be another of ET's creations—a nearly immovable frame with split palm slats. The bed itself was double sized, graced by a single-sized mattress made of wadded cotton with about as much give to it as a wrestling mat. I needed no bedside table. The "leftover" slats, not covered by the mattress, were split bamboo like the walls and afforded a platform for books, flashlight, and candle. My dresser was a stack of those ubiquitous kerosene boxes on which I hung a flowered curtain. I had brought from home a little red fireman's lantern, which I suspended from a nail, and a plastic clothes bag, which served as a closet.

Nobody would have called my bedroom cozy. It was much too big to begin with. I wondered why this, the first house that ET built, was so commodious, while the Santo Domingo one was so cramped. When I lay in bed I could look straight up into the thatch, perhaps fifteen or twenty feet above me. The wood of the furniture and floors was unfinished and had turned a sort of moldy gray. If I had believed I was to spend the rest of my life here I would have been more depressed by it than I was. But I was not settling down—I had agreed to come only temporarily to help Doreen and Barbara—and a few personal touches such as a clean linen cover on the "dresser," an atomizer bottle of Tweed cologne, a few vines in a jar, and some calendar pictures on the wall gave me a feeling of decency. Some of this I described in my letter to Jim. His house, as he described it to me, was similar, but the luxury we enjoyed was space. I had always imagined a "hut." This was a house, and if I had been writing a real estate advertisement, I would have called it "spacious and airy with hand-hewn beams, an informal living room, and a setting of lush tropical landscaping." Someday, perhaps Jim and I would be building a house of our own somewhere in the Ecuadorian rain forest. I had ideas already of how it might look, but had had no occasion to discuss them with him. We were missionaries, each called to his own work for the present.

6

A Church, a School,
and a Language

The Protestant mission work in San Miguel had been set in motion by an Englishman named Wilfred Tidmarsh. He was working with Quichua Indians in the eastern part of Ecuador, known as the Oriente, but visited San Miguel, saw the need of evangelizing the Colorados, and bought property for a mission station. When ET and his wife arrived in Ecuador, Dr. Tidmarsh (he had a PhD in geology) persuaded them and Doreen to settle in San Miguel. No Colorados lived there, or in any village for that matter, for it was their custom to live separately even from one another, scattered here and there as families throughout the forest. San Miguel was as close as a white man could get.

When Dorothy and I arrived there was nothing to show for the Colorado effort. They remained peaceful, tolerant of outsiders, and utterly aloof. But there was a small group of white Christians, Ecuadorians, and Colombians (the latter had fled from the persecution of Protestants in their own country), who met together in what they called an "Assembly." Subscribing to the beliefs of those known in English-speaking countries as "Plymouth Brethren," they purposely did not use the word "church" because they were trying to follow the New Testament literally. "Churches" are mentioned in the New Testament, but the word then did not carry the present connotations of building, denomination, or organization with central authority. "Assembly" seemed a better word. Doreen and Barbara in England, Dorothy and I in the United States, had been identified with such groups. We were not called "members," for all Christians are "members" of the Body of Christ and we eschewed any more narrowly defined membership. There was a Sunday school, begun by Doreen because a child came to her house one Saturday afternoon and asked when there would be a meeting for the children. "Tomorrow," Doreen answered promptly. She had been waiting for ET to take the initiative, because women in the "Assemblies" are expected to keep to the background. Somehow ET, because of his trucks and one thing or another, was not around much on Sundays, so Doreen felt she would be usurping no one's authority if she started a Sunday school.

Sunday school was followed by a worship service, "the breaking of bread," for which the Christians gathered to commemorate the death of Christ. Anything less formal as a religious service could hardly be imagined, but it had, nevertheless its nearly unvarying form or liturgy. The brethren met in the schoolroom, which occupied the ground floor of our house. The benches were arranged in a modified circle, surrounding a table on which were a whole loaf of bread and a cup of wine. No one was assigned to lead the meeting—this was left to the Spirit of God—but everyone knew that the Spirit would never appoint a woman, and only certain of the men. These were recognized as "gifted" although none had had any theological training whatsoever, as was true of the leaders of the early Church. No program was planned, let alone printed up in advance, but an outsider would have observed a remarkable regularity from Sunday to Sunday. A few hymns were sung without accompaniment, not only because no accompaniment was available but also because it was felt that an instrumentalist might be tempted to vanity, or might distract from the true worship of God. One of the brethren, who, it was hoped, was gifted in music, started the singing. He chose the pitch, or perhaps fell upon or plunged into it by accident, and the others took it up in a loud, nasal whine, slowing gradually with each stanza until they ground to a complete halt at the end. Another man then led in prayer, another read a portion of the Bible and added his own extemporaneous commentary. There were usually several hymns, several prayers, several "words" from the Bible (little homilies often referred to as Brother So-and-So's "little word"), before one of the number rose, took up the loaf of bread, broke it in half, and passed it around. Another passed the single cup of wine. Then followed a prayer of thanksgiving and the meeting was over for another week.

It was indeed an unimpressive show for anyone who was not a part of it. A scraggly-looking group of the poor and humble, many barefooted, some of the women nursing babies or fussing with toddlers, the men occasionally going to the window to see what was happening outside or to the door to spit, dogs wandering in and out, children talking—could God be present here? Would Almighty God dwell in the midst of such a company? I myself asked this question when the physical appearances threatened all spiritual sensibility. The whole thing often seemed farcical. Nevertheless, I saw in the little gathering, in my saner moments, a reality that could not fail to move me. Here, in the greatest simplicity, a few true believers had come together to give testimony to their belief. They saw through a glass darkly, but what they saw was the true Light, and I pictured the Colorados, someday, joining in worship with the others, learning to sing and pray, partaking of the bread and wine, becoming followers of that Light. In the years since, as I have participated in other communion services, as different as they could be in outward appearance, I have remembered those services in San Miguel. As regards the setting, the music, the degree of understanding on the part of the majority, the command of language of those who spoke or prayed, or any helps toward atmosphere, sensitivity, or taste in worship, the San Miguel church left everything to be desired. But Almighty God does come and in fact dwell with men. And He, when He was God manifest in the flesh, left a simple command, "This do in remembrance of me." Obedience to that command is possible nearly anywhere, anytime, by any who are willing. It does not require much in the way of visible trappings, of emotional enthusiasm, or of intellectual vigor. "It hits below the intellect," I heard a priest once say.

So it was this San Miguel assembly that was the real heart of our life together.

Ripples sometimes disturbed the calm face of our ecclesiastical pond. One such was the arrival of a young man in the clearing on a Sunday morning, announcing that he was a graduate of a Bible institute. Although he was received kindly, as a Christian brother, he was regarded with consternation when he proceeded to take over both the Sunday school class and the worship service. He considered it his due to be allowed to minister in this fashion, and no one stopped him, but the brethren gathered in groups afterward and shook their heads. That a man could complete the required course in a Bible school and remain so ignorant of New Testament principles of church polity puzzled them, but they did not allow themselves to be led away from the pattern that they believed in. The young man moved on without being invited to come back.

The other weekly service of the church was a women's meeting. Nothing during that year in San Miguel impressed itself more vividly on my memory than the sight of Doreen, dressed up for the meeting in one of her better (that is to say, less faded, less sagging) cotton print dresses, wearing sandals, white bobby socks, and a head scarf (for women covered their heads for all church meetings), standing atop a fence post in front of our house, swinging a big, clanging school bell with all her might and main. No one could say that any of the women failed to come to the meeting because she forgot about it. There stood Doreen, a symbol of conscience and duty, but exhibiting at the same time a recklessness and gaiety, perched on her pedestal, rending the silence of the hot, sleepy afternoon with the peal of her bell, calling the hardworking women away from their siesta, summoning them to hear the Word of the Lord. They came, heads duly covered, children clinging to their skirts, and prayed together (this was their chance to pray aloud, for no men were present), and then listened as best they could to Doreen's Bible teaching.

The work of the church came first in our minds, but the work of the school was also important. The government at that time had not gotten around to providing schools in the jungle, and generally granted permission to anyone who wanted to do so. Our school was the first in San Miguel, but a Roman Catholic priest soon arrived to start his own on the other side of the clearing. Life was at once sharply divided between *Católicos* and *Evangélicos*, as the Protestants were usually called. It was strange that the church ("the Assembly"), which had existed for several years, had never polarized the groups. No Catholic church as such had ever been formed, but the school was taken seriously and opposition began.

Marta, a Catholic herself, had no difficulty working with the *Evangélicos*. It was her job and she had no ax to grind. Dorothy was officially the principal of the school and also saw to getting books, pencils, and slates and cleaning the schoolroom. Marta taught the three Rs in a customary rote method, and all day we heard the drone of the children reciting aloud things like "the rivers of Italy are the following . . ." and "the personal pronouns are these . . ." There was something heartbreaking to me in hearing these recitations shouted so earnestly for so long by these poor little

52

children. They came from homes where there was no such thing as a book or a map or a piece of paper nor anyplace to put such a thing if it were given them, and they would probably spend their lives tilling a small patch of jungle, but perhaps they would learn to read the Bible and that would make tilling the soil all the more worthwhile.

I was glad Doreen's and Dorothy's jobs did not fall to me. Barbara was in charge of making contacts with the Colorados, and it was my job to get ahold of the Colorado language, by far the most interesting task of all. If I could figure out how to write it down, someday we would be able to translate the Bible for the Colorado Indians. That's what I had come to do. It was the kind of work I believed God had called me to do while I was still a junior in college.

The idea of a calling presupposes several major religious convictions without which none of us four foreign women would have come to San Miguel de los Colorados. We believed, of course, in God. We believed Him to be a personal God who "calls" people—individuals—and makes Himself and His will known to them in many different ways. He sends people who believe in Him to others who do not. In other words, the Good News, which is the gospel, is meant for everyone, and the Colorados of Ecuador's jungle had a right to hear it.

These were the fundamentals. For me there was also a deep conviction that God blesses those who obey Him and works things out in beautiful, demonstrable ways for those who have given themselves to do His work. I had heard many sermons about the coldness and disobedience of the church. I knew that millions had never heard of Christ because so few were willing to go and tell them. But here I was, called, prayed for, provided with every material need. My home church had done its job. I, so far as I knew, was here in obedience and my purpose was to do God's work. There was every reason to expect that God would grant us success.

7

Jungle Housekeeping

Missionary life, in my mind's eye before I went to Ecuador, comprised green jungle, thatch-roofed houses, and Indians. San Miguel fit the picture well, but what I had not seen in my imagination was what would be involved in putting those elements into some kind of working relationship. What was involved, I found, took up about nine-tenths of our time.

There was the matter of water. Our supply was a small river at least three hundred yards away, across the *plaza* and down a steep, usually muddy bank. People swam, bathed, washed clothes, watered their animals, and washed their chamber pots in this river. Most of them, I think, used it as a latrine as well. We were told that the latrine part was customarily downriver, and we counted heavily on that. Edelina, the teenaged daughter of one of the Christian men in the assembly, worked for us a few hours of every day. She saved us most of the labor of lugging the water from the river, but it was surprising how much time we spent in dipping water from buckets, carrying it in pitchers or pots or basins to wherever we needed it, and then in lugging the slop water to the back porch, from which we flung it out onto the yard. Faucets and drains, of which we had none, began to seem like miracles of ingenuity.

I had survived living in an Ecuadorian home in Quito where the drinking water was never boiled, although according to other missionaries, "typhoid germs just pour out of the faucets." When the kitchen was being remodeled, I had even survived eating from dishes washed in a duck pond that had ducks still swimming merrily in it. Given the latrine situation in San Miguel, however, I went along with the general missionary consensus that drinking water ought to be boiled. The books on tropical survival said for twenty minutes at least. This turned out to be much too much trouble—keeping the fire in the *fogón* going was a demanding exercise at best, and to light a gasoline pressure stove just to boil water was an expensive nuisance. We ended up bringing it to a boil, allowing the sediment to settle, and hoping for the best. Sometimes we collected rainwater from the thatched roof, but that had a funny color and an even funnier taste, probably because it was full of penicillin and other gratuitous nourishment.

We had to boil milk, too, which anyone who has tried it knows it is a good deal more trouble than boiling water. It has a way of doing nothing for a long time, and the minute you turn your back it swells over the top, down over the sides of the pot, and extinguishes the fire. The sudden cessation of the pressure stove's roar, the nauseating odor, and the quiet dripping that let us know that the milk had boiled over were an almost daily occurrence. We salvaged what was left, plucked out the ribbons of skin that had formed on top, covered it to keep the flies out, and then tried to decide whether it was worth drinking since there was no way to get it cold.

Then there were the simple little things that, for safety's sake, one ought not to overlook. They only take a minute. Like washing lettuce. "Avoid raw vegetables" is a good advice for a tourist, but if you are going to live in a place (it was living we were aiming for, not mere tropical survival), you want raw vegetables sometimes. The book said to dip everything, lettuce included, in boiling water for a few seconds. This could be counted on usually to kill amoeba and always to kill one's zest for salad. We tried what another book suggested: soak lettuce in water (boiled cooled water it had to be—and there went another precious quart) with a few drops of permanganate added. Yet other books declared that this treatment would do nothing to hurt either ourselves or the germs, but we kept up the practice most of the time as it made us feel we were doing something.

Unpasteurized butter occasionally came by horseback from Santo Domingo. This, too, we were told, must be boiled. Here we drew the line. Some risks obviously had to be taken. We kept it submerged in a jar of saltwater to keep it from spoiling, and it lasted a week or more. When it was gone, we used jam on our bread—jam which we had to make. We concocted sweets out of whatever we could find. When there were oranges, we bought a hundred for thirty cents. Sometimes we made jam of apple peelings and cores or green papayas. There was no such thing as prepared foods. We never just opened a can of something for supper. Each meal had to be planned and prepared, especially taking into account the tastes of our schoolteacher Marta, who had been accustomed to two full-course meals a day besides breakfast. We ate whatever we had, often the same menu twice in a day in order to use up leftovers immediately (we had no refrigerator to store them in). One of the great joys was pineapple. Sometimes there were none at all, but often there were huge quantities of them, big and sweet and running with juice, and we could buy them for three or four cents apiece. Rice, eggs, beans, and bananas were the foods we could count on all the time.

One day I heard that they would be killing a pig the next morning. It did not at first occur to me that this was an event at which I had better be present. It meant meat, and if I wanted to buy some, I had better be there when the animal was killed. The whole population of San Miguel was alerted at six o'clock by the hideous shrieks and squeals of the doomed creature, and we hurried to the spot with plates, pots, and money in hand. The flaying and cutting up was done with amazing speed, and soon a huge vat of lard was bubbling and popping over an open fire and people were throwing in pieces of plantain and manioc to deep-fry. There were cracklings as well, and I bought a handful of these in a newspaper package. I carried home a pale gray chunk of pork, unidentifiable as to its cut and stuck about with bristles, for which I had paid fifteen cents a pound. We had a wonderful breakfast that morning of fried pork, cracklings, roasted plantains, and coffee, a pleasant change from oatmeal and boiled milk.

Bread making was another major project. It was hard to get flour to San Miguel. It was harder to keep it from becoming moldy or weevil-infested. It was hard to get yeast and keep it fresh. It was quite a task to mix and knead on the narrow board we had for a counter, but the worst difficulty was the oven. The small, round, aluminum contraption fit over the top of the pressure stove. It held only a single loaf, a round one, and the first few times I made the loaf too big, so that it rose and lifted the top off the oven, cooling the oven and spilling down over the sides of the pan. In time we learned to make the loaves the proper size, but there was no putting the bread in the oven and forgetting about it for an hour. One of us had to hover over it continually, trying to keep the temperamental pressure stove from burning the bread to a cinder or from fizzling out altogether.

We also had a pressure cooker. It seemed a godsend at first, but you had to have a stove that fit with it. Our stove did not. Our sanctification was rigorously tried as we sought to tenderize our meat or beans in this civilized pot. It worked for a while, but one day, the stove being too hot for it, it blew its safety valve right through the thatched roof. It was lost forever, so the Lord delivered us from that temptation.

Wood was another thing. It was sometimes green, sometimes rain-soaked as well. We never seemed to get ahead enough to dry it properly, for this would have taken months or even years in so humid a climate. We were forever nursing reluctant fires that sizzled and hissed. The sound of Edelina's fan seemed to go most of the day, and cooking was always a very smoky and slow business.

Edelina washed our clothes in a tub with an old-fashioned scrub board, which was quite new-fashioned to her who had been used to pounding clothes on the rocks in the river. She fetched buckets of water, heated it in the tub by building a fire underneath, and used detergent that we were able to buy in Santo Domingo, or lacking that, bars of blue soap fifteen inches long which she cut into manageable cakes. The clothes were hung on a line in the yard or under the back porch, but rarely dried in a single day because of the heavy mist and relatively short intervals of sunlight. Dorothy or I would usually have to bring them in in the late afternoon, drape them about the furniture, and carry them out again the next morning.

Then there was ironing. We had a gasoline pressure iron which was as infuriating as the pressure cooker and the pressure stove. It was always getting clogged, and had to be prodded with a special pin, whereupon it would roar and pop with flames for a few minutes just as you got nicely started on a blouse, and then die ignominiously as you were about to finish collar and cuffs. By the time you reamed it, filled it, primed and pumped it again, the collar and cuffs had dried. You might get a garment beautifully ironed once in a while, hang it up with satisfaction and pride, and find that after a wet jungle night it had unironed itself. We began to understand how Doreen and Barbara had come to terms with wrinkles.

None of us felt sorry for ourselves for having to cope with inconveniences. Inconvenience belonged to missionary life. The proportion of time, however, that was consumed with these temporal matters bothered me. When I was fiddling with the stove, I felt that I ought to be working on the language, the real work I had come for. But what perversity of my nature was it that made me put off the language work even when the dishes were being done by Edelina, the clothes were hung on the line, and the bread had been baked? I would hie myself over to the study and sharpen pencils. I would find that the desk was littered with scorched bugs from the lamp the night before, and would have to set about a major cleaning operation. I would rearrange file cards and dash off a few letters I wanted to have ready in case someone offered to carry mail to Santo Domingo. "As soon as I get this stuff out of the way, I can settle into the task," I told myself. It was a monumental struggle every day for me to get at the brain work instead of dawdling with physical work. The awful truth was that I really preferred the housekeeping. I loved order and neatness and organization but I did not like to concentrate. After an hour or two of sheer effort of willpower to stick at the job, I was relieved when I had to go back to the house and check Edelina's progress with the lunch.

"I the Lord have called thee" . . . these words were always in the back of my mind. I was sure they were true. The reduction of the Colorado language was a divinely appointed task and I must do it.

8

An Unwritten Language

Colorado was an unwritten language—one of the two thousand or so without a single page of the Bible that I had heard about as a college student. This had stunned me. Could I perhaps help to reduce this figure? I had received good marks in language studies at school and had a certain knack for mimicry. It looked as though God was directing me toward language work rather than medical work. Other things conspired to steer me in this direction, and between my junior and senior years in college, I changed my major to classical Greek, with a view to using the Greek in the translation of the New Testament. After graduation, I took a summer course in linguistics at the University of Oklahoma, under the auspices of an organization known as the Wycliffe Bible Translators or the Summer Institute of Linguistics. I completed the required course, but like most others who take it, did not become a part of the organization.

The first thing one must do to learn an unwritten language is to find an "informant," someone willing to help, someone with enough patience to sit for long periods saying the same things over and over while the foreigner struggles to write them down. This is an exceedingly boring task. For the Indian, who had never had to learn his own language (so far as he can recall), it is impossible to fathom the difficulty this otherwise reasonably intelligent adult has in *hearing* what the Indian says. The foreigner can't hear it, he can't reproduce it, and he can't understand what it means. He is making strange marks on paper all the time, which seems quite beside the point, and tomorrow he will make the same hilarious blunders, peer intently into the informant's mouth while he speaks, and ask the same imbecilic questions. Not many people want a job like that.

But I felt certain that with the help of Doreen and Barbara I would soon find one who would do it for a modest price. On the Saturday after my arrival in San Miguel, I saw my first Colorado Indian. I was hanging some sheets out on the line and happened to look up at just the right moment. Out of the forest on the eastern side of the clearing rode a man on horseback. He seemed to be wearing a vermilion-red visored helmet. As he came closer, I could see on top of this a ring of white cotton. His face, arms, and all I could see of his body were painted brilliant red. There were black horizontal stripes beginning at his forehead and painted all the way to his toes, and in between the stripes, black polka dots. He wore a black-and-white striped skirt reaching not much below his hips, and over his shoulders he had flung several bright yellow and turquoise cotton scarves. He rode straight to Doreen's gate, hitched his small horse, and walked boldly up to her door. She came out, greeted him, and as I approached, introduced him to me.

His straight carriage and beautifully proportioned body had given him the appearance of height, but I saw now that he was not more than five and half feet tall. He smiled, revealing black-stained teeth and tongue. His lips, too, were stained blue-black. We shook hands, and if his hands seemed small and hard to me, mine must have seemed startlingly huge and uncalloused to him.

I asked Doreen (in English) if we might broach the subject of language study, and after a few pleasantries, she edged toward the business with great delicacy. She spoke Spanish to him, which I understood, and he replied, speaking a strange truncated Spanish, very polite, very devious, and completely noncommittal. He would be back, he said. He only wanted some pills now, he was going to town, but he would be back. We gave him the pills, and he mounted his horse and rode off, a flaming spectacle of red, yellow, and turquoise, atop a red-brown pony, disappearing once more into the green scrim of the forest on the far side of the clearing. That helmet now, I asked Doreen—what on earth did an Indian need a helmet for?

"Helmet!" she shrieked. "That's his hair!" She explained that Colorado men plastered their hair with a thick mixture of Vaseline and *achiote*, a red dye taken from the seedpod of a jungle tree.

Perhaps a dozen more Indians rode through the *plaza* that day on their way to Santo Domingo. They always went to town, Doreen said, on Saturdays. They would lounge around the town square, drink the night away, and we could look for them back again, drunken and toppling off their horses, on Sunday. We waylaid several and asked if they would come next week to work for the señorita who wanted to learn their talk. All were amiable and said they would certainly come.

During the week that followed I trekked hopefully with Doreen or Barbara and talked with whomever I found at home. It became clear that no one really intended to work for me. The truth was that Colorados never worked for anybody. Some of them, in fact, actually had white men working for them. They were wealthy because of the export of bananas and *achiote*, the latter for the coloring of margarine. Money meant very little. They had lived near white men for centuries and had had plenty of opportunity to assess the white man's way of life. A good hard look was enough. They did not like it. They chose to keep to their own way, spending money only for a few things like salt, kerosene, Vaseline, cotton thread, and gin. They had not the slightest urge to dress like white men, or build houses like theirs, or submit themselves to their economic slavery, and nothing would persuade them otherwise.

I was embarrassed and offended by this higher criticism. Nothing had prepared me for it. I was here to help and these people would not be helped. I had no doubt that God was on my side, and this was a secret satisfaction. Someday God and I would show these proud, independent Indians that we had plans for them, plans that they would not ultimately succeed in thwarting. One way or another (God would show me the way), I would get ahold of the language, make it my own, harness it into an alphabet, and make the Indians readers and writers. This would surely happen. But getting them to acknowledge that they were living in "bondage, sorrow, and night" was going to be a lengthy process. They were not interested, not in the least, in our definition of liberation. Besides, time was always on their side. White men came and went with their plans and projects. They were a nuisance while they were around, but the Indians knew how to keep out of their way and live their hidden lives.

I did what any Christian in trouble would do: I prayed. The task was impossible, it couldn't even begin without an informant, so I started with that. I asked specifically for an informant. I was sure that God could budge even a Colorado, if He wanted to, especially if that Colorado's soul's salvation depended on it. The question of whether my prayer was according to His will did not (as it often does) seem a difficult one then. The work I hoped to do was God's work. It was His Word that was at stake—"Faith cometh by hearing, and hearing by the word of God" (Rom. 10:17 KJV). I was His worker. It was all clear and simple. My prayer was as free from selfish and impure motives as any I had ever prayed. I had God's written promises of help, such as that in Isaiah 50:7, "The Lord GOD will help me; therefore shall I not be confounded; therefore have I set my face like a flint, and I know that I shall not be ashamed" (KJV).

The prayer was answered. A middle-aged Ecuadorian named Don Macario had been coming to the Assembly meetings. His credentials were unparalleled. A white man of Spanish-speaking parentage, he had grown up on a hacienda with Colorado children and was completely bilingual.

Hence, he was even better qualified to help me than any Indian would have been. He was, just at this time, out of work. When he learned of my need, he was willing to work for me, and at a price that I could afford to pay. He was, above all, a Christian. The ultimate aim of a Bible translation interested him because he had been wishing for some way to serve the Lord. It was the perfect answer for both of us, better than we could have imagined, "exceeding abundantly above all" that I had asked or thought.

We agreed on a regular program of study, and Doreen let me have one of the little rooms of her house to work in, since the schoolchildren's racket made concentration impossible in our house. I set up a table and chairs, got out notebooks, file-cards, and pencils, and Macario came in for one hour every morning and sometimes for another hour in the afternoon. He had no idea of teaching the language, of course, but he could answer my questions, and I had learned at school in Oklahoma what you are supposed to ask.

I learned that the Indians called their own language *Tsah-fihki*, "the language of the people." The second vowel in the word was a "voiceless" one pronounced in a whisper, and I soon found that the language was full of these. It took several weeks to find out why Macario was not satisfied with my pronunciation of *sha*, meaning "let's go." There were actually two syllables, the first being a voiceless *i* pronounced like the English word "he," only in a whisper: *he-sha*. There were things called glottal stops, which we pronounce but never write in English. (All words beginning with vowels really begin with glottal stops in English. The negative *hn-n* has one in the middle.) In Colorado you have to write glottal stops.

I made neat charts of *Tsahfihki* sounds and syllables, shuffling them around to work out systems and patterns.

To figure out the divisions between words was nearly as absorbing as working out the plot of a mystery story. At first I wrote only what we called "sequences," making divisions between them by guesswork. Macario had never thought about what constituted a single word. He spoke, but did not analyze, the language. He thought in phrases, as we all do, until we read and write a language. He would repeat phrases to me, but it was next to impossible to get him to say a noun or a verb by itself. Little by little, by endless charting and comparing and filing, I began to recognize what were probably prefixes, infixes, and suffixes, and these gave me a clue to where word borders were, and I began to draw lines. If Macario did not recognize a single word out of its context, he certainly did not recognize syllables by themselves and could not identify the meanings of suffixes, but he could think of examples of where they occurred, and I wrote each example on a separate slip of paper and filed it. A second-grader might, for example, have a hard time telling his teacher what *-ing* means in English, but he might think of words like eating and running and swimming. Eventually the linguist would find a label for *-ing*.

Next I would try to identify the class of suffix or prefix I was working on. Could it appear only with verbs? With nouns as well? Did it occur before or after another suffix? Had it anything to do with the gender of the subject, the shape of the object, or perhaps the time or mode or voice? Did a pronoun such as "we" include you and me, them and me, or you and them and me?

Orthography would be another part of the job. Every sound I could possibly hear or see (in the case of voiceless vowels I could sometimes recognize them only by seeing the lip and tongue position rather than by hearing) I wrote down, using the phonetic symbols, but I had to try to reduce the *Tsahfihki* alphabet to the fewest possible letters that would adequately represent the sounds.

In English, for example, we have only one written form of the letter *t*, although it has two pronunciations. These are "phonetic," which means they have different sounds as the *t* in "top" (aspirated) and the *t* in "stop" (unaspirated). They are not, however, "phonemic," that is, they need not be written differently in the English alphabet because aspirated *t*'s occur only in certain positions, distinct from that of unaspirated *t*'s. A simple rule can guide the foreigner in pronunciation. But the English alphabet has many features that are not nearly so neat. There are several pronunciations for each of the five vowels, and this difficulty is compounded by the many vowel combinations—take *ou*, for example, in the words "tough," "though," "through," "thought," and "plough."

We wanted to avoid problems like this for the Colorados. If we were ever going to teach them to read their language (and it would be of no use to reduce their language to writing if they were never going to read it), we wanted it to be as simple as possible. When I reduced the alphabet to the smallest number of symbols needed, I had a "phonemic" alphabet. I then began to write a simple primer that Barbara and Doreen could use to teach the Colorados to read.

Besides being an invaluable informant, Macario ran a little store for us. We tried to think of ways to bring the Indians to our clearing as much as possible, and a store seemed a good idea. We also thought it might keep some of them from going to Santo Domingo, where they sometimes were robbed and nearly always got drunk.

Macario was in the shop one day and I was sitting in my study room nearby, waiting for him to begin our session. Two old Colorado women came into the study, dressed in brightly colored striped skirts, beads, and red paint. Their hair hung down, long and straight, over their bare breasts. Each had a mirror hanging around her neck on a piece of string. They wanted me to come with them to the schoolroom in the other house. I could not make out why, but followed them over and they pointed to the folding organ we used for our meetings.

"Can you play?" they asked in Spanish.

"Yes."

"Then play!" they said.

I played some simple hymn tunes while they sat and twiddled their toes and ran their hands through their hair. When I thought they had had enough, I stopped playing, but they begged for more and I played until my legs ached from pumping. Macario came in and I asked him if he thought I might take the old women's picture. He talked to them for a long time in *Tsahfihki*, assuring them that the camera would not make them sick, and they consented. Then I sat with them on the veranda, listening to their talk, sorting out of it several words that I could write down.

I told Barbara about the delightful hour I had spent with them.

"Oh, yes, I know those two!" Barbara said. "Sporting old sticks, aren't they?"

That priceless British manner of speaking never failed to delight me. Barbara's description of the Indian women seemed to me a perfect one as well for her and Doreen. They took their work, but not themselves, seriously, keeping always a stiff upper lip, treating the rest of us—Americans, Indians, or Ecuadorians—as fellow players in a great game.

I don't recall hearing either complain of physical hardships of any kind. There was a remarkable unself-conscious courage and toughness about these two women that inspired me and, although I am sure that neither was aware of it, made me treat my own troubles more lightly.

9

The Neighbors

Each morning as Marta rang our school bell, the priest rang his across the *plaza*. Several pupils who had started in our school had drifted into the Catholic school. In those days serious differences had arisen between Catholics and Protestants, leading to conflicts resulting, in some cases in Colombia, in murder. Not surprisingly, we *Bankelistas* (the Indians' garbled pronunciation of *Evangelistas*) were wary, as were *los Catolicos*. It was not easy for either group to trust the other. The teacher in the priest's school was a former nun who had switched to Protestantism and back again to Catholicism. She felt that we foreign women were guilty of hypocrisy, heresy, and a lack of discipline. Perhaps we would have felt the same about them. Our church meetings were simple in the extreme—we sang gospel songs, listened to the reading of the Bible, and prayed without kneeling down. Ours was a church where, to Carlota, everything was missing.

"I have founded a proper school," she wrote in a pamphlet she distributed. "I am confident that our holy religion will be known, loved, and respected. The school now has twenty-three children, may all be for the glory of God and for our good Mother, the Virgin Mary."

It was true that she had twenty-three children. We had about a dozen. We saw little of her, but heard often that she was doing all she could to discourage people from sending their children to our school or from attending our meetings. She was a woman of great spirit—young, vigorous, black-haired, and with high coloring—and whenever we did catch a glimpse of her she seemed to be in a great rush, her black habit (for she dressed as a nun again) billowing behind her and her head thrown back. It looked to me as if we were locked in combat between truth and falsehood from which falsehood was likely to emerge victorious. But Doreen took no such view. She was as much a crusader as Carlota, equally convinced about her vocation and truth of her message. Her conviction that Carlota would not trouble us for long gave heart to the rest of us.

When we had our evening prayer meeting, we could hear the Rosary being said across the clearing. A child who had been dozing on the bench suddenly sat up and began to giggle. Then in a loud clear voice he said, "Ah, listen to how the priest sings!" It was strange to a little boy who knew only our gospel songs.

Everyone was amused but I recoiled. Even the sight of the priest and nuns across the clearing made me uneasy. Their work, it seemed to me, could not be the work of God. Would it finally vanquish ours? We struggled to keep a grip on those whom we thought of as "our" people.

Another neighbor, one we thought of as part of our missionary family, was Soledad. She was an old Colorado woman who, for some reason, spoke enough Spanish for us to understand and communicate with her. She cooked for Barbara. One morning she sent word that she was afraid to come to the clearing by herself. She lived perhaps an hour's walk away. I was free, and went to get her. As we came back along the trail she chattered away in her odd Spanish with a Colorado intonation pattern. She had a machete in her hand, and used it as we walked to hack at an overhanging branch, or cut a few steps for her feet in the bank of a stream. I was wondering what had made her afraid on this particular morning—she had always come by herself before—but I did not ask. Occasionally she lifted a leaf with the machete to make sure there were no snakes hiding underneath. We sat down for a moment on a log and she scratched her gnat-bitten legs with the blunt side of the implement.

"The priest said, 'Don't work for those devils,'" she said suddenly.

"For us?" I asked.

"For you. You evil foreign spirits." She held up a small foot and slowly scraped the mud from it with her machete. "'You will be cursed if you disobey,' he told me."

"And do you believe him?" I asked.

"His word is strong," she said. "Today I will cook, tomorrow who knows?"

Our next-door neighbors on one side were a white Ecuadorian family who ran a cantina, a small saloon that produced a great deal of noise at night. We would watch the arrival of kegs and boxes by mule or donkey, and an odd assortment of men who came and went, but we hardly glimpsed the residents themselves. I wondered if we should go over there. It was the wrong sort of place, full of the wrong sort of people, but what sort, after all, was our gospel meant for? On the other hand, what would people say if the foreign señoritas were seen visiting the cantina? I remembered, however, from the missionary books of my childhood, pictures of redoubtable females storming saloons in the name of the Lord. They never stopped to worry about what people would say. They had something to say themselves. We had enough work to do, work that had been specifically assigned to each of us. We must be careful not to spread ourselves too thin. None of us ever went to the cantina, but at night I would lie in bed listening to the din, and I would pray for them. One night we were awakened by a burst of sweet song, accompanied by a guitar and maracas. A group of young men stood by our gate and sang tragic songs of love. Dorothy and I were not sure how to respond to a Spanish serenade—to appear and thank them, or to pretend that we hadn't noticed? I think we thanked them from the dark windows of our house.

On the other side of Barbara's house lived an extremely poor Colombian family of Protestants who had fled their country because of persecution by the Catholics. They had brought almost nothing with them except their faith and a great willingness to work. Edelina was the daughter of this family, and through her we came to know how they lived.

They had two rooms in their board house. Eight people lived in these rooms, and their furniture consisted of two wooden boxes, one board, and eight straw mats for sleeping. They also owned eight plates and spoons, three cooking pots, one large knife, four blankets, and a Bible. I think that was all, except for their scruffy clothes. No one in the family had shoes. They spent their days working in the plantain plantations that belonged to others. They had no diversions except reading the Bible. They had no oven and no money to buy bread, so their menu consisted of plantains—roasted, cooked in ashes, boiled—three times a day. The few *sucres* they earned were spent on kerosene, salt, and beans.

Poverty took on a new meaning for me when I came to know this family. Compared with them, the Colorados (the "poor Indians," as I had thought) were vastly wealthy, but so far as I could tell the Colombians did not think of themselves as destitute. They were literate Christians, devout and spiritually discerning. The father of the family, Don Miguel, was a leader in the Assembly, a man rich in faith. It was a healthy thing for us when we felt any deprivation (such as when the iron refused to function, or the typewriter ribbon got moldy) to take stock of Don Miguel's household.

One of the gayest and liveliest additions to the life of the clearing was Vicente. He was a Colorado boy whom we guessed to be about seven, who lived with Barbara. His grandfather was a witch doctor of much renown, and the Indians came even from the high Sierra to be treated by him. Vicente's stepfather, who had a new wife and was anxious to be free of the responsibility of his dead wife's son, had consented to let Barbara take Vicente and put him in school.

This was a new departure altogether, since no Colorado had ever gone to school. Barbara hoped that Vicente would open the way.

The child lacked any hint of self-consciousness or guile. His black eyes looked straight at you and would twinkle in a most disconcerting way, as if he saw with perfect clarity anything you might be trying to hide. He spoke Spanish haltingly when he first came, but picked it up with astonishing ease along with a few English phrases. I could not resist taking advantage of his gift for mimicry, and to tease Doreen and Barbara I taught him to say "overalls" exactly as the British say it. He learned to say "holy water" with the intonation of an Anglican priest and one day came struggling up our stairway with a bucket of water, shouting "*Ve, señorita, yo le traje un balde de* [Look, señorita, I brought you a bucket of] *holy wootah!*"

One night when I was humming to myself, Barbara found Vicente listening spellbound. The Colorados have no song in their language and no idea of singing (though they do love music and make remarkable bamboo marimbas). After this, he would often ask one or the other of us to sing for him.

I remember how he chortled with glee when Doreen brought back a pair of leather shoes for him from Santo Domingo. He had never had a pair on his feet in his life, and he clumped back and forth in our living room, showing them to us, walking with toes out instead of in as he was used to. When he came he owned no clothes except his striped Colorado skirt, which Barbara wanted him to wear all the time, for she, like the rest of us, had no desire to disrupt the Indian culture. But Vicente begged for "real clothes," and was given a pair of overalls and a T-shirt, the latter nearly always worn inside out and backward. Thus he was "spoiled," not simply in being given what he asked for, but because his Indian identity was gone. He saw the Colorado skirt as a thing to be despised, and although his own people despised the overalls, he loved them. He was not of his people any longer. He lived a new life, in a class by himself, neither a foreigner, nor an Ecuadorian, nor an Indian. This raised the question we struggled with all the time we were missionaries: how to make *Indian* (not American or British) Christians. How were we to live among them and not change a thing except their attitude toward God? We did not see what was happening to Vicente at the time. He was only a little boy, and instead of his providing us with the Colorado viewpoint, we, willy-nilly, quickly gave him ours.

10

Jungle Trails

No diversion was more welcomed, nothing so exhilarated us missionary women, as a call to us from someone in need. The first such emergency that I remember came on a Sunday, when word reached us in a morning meeting of a Colorado woman with malaria. After lunch Doreen and I saddled up the two old nags, hers and Barbara's, with such tack as we had. For people who had no mode of transportation other than horseback, we had given far too little care and thought to our equipment. There was only one blanket, which was put on whichever horse had the worst saddle sores. There was one pair of stirrups, which Doreen said I must use, since I had not done much bareback riding. Only one horse had a halter, one of the cinches had been mended with a piece of jungle vine, and both of us used a frayed length of rope for a bridle. To the

Colorados, whose horses were sleek and well fitted out, we were certainly a poor show.

It was a rare, sunny afternoon. We had very few of these, for the deep hollow where we lived between the Pacific Ocean and the Andes was usually filled with heavy mist and cloud, or rain. There were no mosquitoes or gnats that day, there was a breeze, and the trail was dry. We were very happy, and Doreen had the added pleasure of leading the way for the new and inexperienced missionary. She knew how to saddle the horse, what medicines to take along (she asked me to wear the stethoscope around my neck), she knew the trail, and she knew the family of the sick woman.

The great advantage of traveling on horseback instead of on foot was that you were free to look around. On foot one had to keep one's eyes firmly fixed on the trail in front, watching for snakes, holes to fall into, slippery roots, fire ants, or whatever perils and pitfalls there might be. On horseback, one could leave all that to the horse.

As I rode along I was reminded of the pictures in elementary geography books that depicted the earth during the formation of coal. I had always found those pictures so much more fascinating than those showing factories, dams, resources, raw materials, principal exports, and aerial views of deltas and things. The giant trees, the giant-sized leaves of the lower plants, the tree ferns and air plants, all of these things laced about with lianas, made me feel as if I had come not only to a foreign country and a strange people but to a different aeon of time. It would have been appropriate to see a pterodactyl suddenly flap overhead, or the absurd small head of a diplodocus peer on its snaky neck round the bend of a trail.

We did see enormous butterflies, some of them eight inches across. They would float up around the horses as we rode, and sail gently off into the dim light of the forest, but never so gently that we were able to catch them. Once I saw a huge purple one with gold on the underside of its wings, so lovely a sight that I thought perhaps I had seen a vision.

There were many fallen logs that had rotted along the trail, and in some of them tropical plants were growing, arranged as beautifully as if someone had set them there like window boxes for us to enjoy.

We left the main trail and took one so narrow that we often had to lie flat along the horses' necks in order to avoid being lifted up, like Absalom, between heaven and earth. At last, we reached the house, built of bamboo slats with a thatched roof and eaves so wide at one end that they formed a covered veranda. We expected to find the sick woman lying near death. In fact, she had gone visiting. The other members of the family whooped and shouted themselves hoarse, and at length she appeared. Doreen's examination indicated that hers was a variety of malaria that gave a high fever on alternate days, and this was not a fever day. In the house there was a slatted table and a platform for sleeping that had straw mats with red stains from *achiote* on it. Someone fanned up a fire and boiled some water in a small blackened clay pot, and Doreen sterilized her hypodermic needle and syringe and gave the woman an injection. This was a great satisfaction to all. The Indians found the medicine, visibly flowing out of the syringe into the living flesh, highly reassuring; on the other occasions when Doreen would refuse to administer an injection, knowing that it was not called for, they felt insulted. Why should they put up with these foreigners in their midst if the foreigners were going to be unmanageable? In general the Indians could be counted upon to answer all calls and fulfill any petition with goodwill, but now and then their will was crossed and the foreigners began to look like enemies.

We rode home in twilight and then starlight with the weird shadows around us, the squeak of the saddle, the soft sound of the horses' hoofs, the calls of birds and insects giving a voice to the night. I was holding the rope bridle in one hand and two eggs that had been given to us in payment in the other, expecting at any moment to crush them in my palm if the horse happened to lurch. We found the lantern lit in Doreen's house when we reached the clearing, and Barbara was making tea.

On another occasion, one evening after supper we heard a Colorado call outside. A man had come to say that his brother had broken his leg and was dying. Would Doreen come? She asked me to accompany her in case she needed help in pulling it to set the bone. Any Indian would have known as much about it as I did, but I was more than willing for the adventure. The two Colorados were terribly agitated, for no one they knew of had ever broken a bone and surely it must be a fatal thing. Doreen reassured them, we quickly donned what passed for riding clothes, packed up a few supplies, and set out. The Indians had brought horses for us. Mine was an excellent little creature that moved smoothly along in the dark, so that although he wore no stirrups I had no trouble keeping my seat. It was a beautiful night, with the moon showing through lovely clouds. The horses knew the trail but we had to watch our heads, as the horses, following their usual habit, skirted the edge of it. We were joined at the first house we came to by four men, all of them well painted, solemn, and silent, conscious of the importance of the occasion. Two were carrying Eveready flashlights and went ahead on foot to light the way. The bad part of the journey was yet to come. Not far beyond the house the two Indians on horseback who were in front of us suddenly vanished as if they had fallen into a hole. There was silence, then the sound of a sliding plunge, a crash, the splash of water. The flashlight beams did not reach to the bottom of the ravine, but there was nothing for us to do but follow. *Here goes*, I thought, hanging on to the back of the wooden saddle and digging my knees into the horse's shoulder blades with all my might to keep from plummeting over his head. I held my breath as we dropped into the blackness. The horse pitched violently from side to side, trying to find footholds as his hoofs hit rocks, holes, or tree roots. When he could hold no more we slid for what seemed forever. A sudden wrench and he gained a foothold once more, but the momentum sent us tearing and twisting into the river with a great splash. It was shallow, and we were soon across it and struggling up the steep bank on the other side, my fingers wound tightly into his mane to keep from slithering down over his flanks.

"There are three more of these," announced one of the Indians laconically, and we braced ourselves, not knowing how soon to expect the next. His count was wrong, however. There were twelve more, some worse than the first, but I began to trust the little horse and to get some of the thrill of riding a roller coaster.

At about eleven o'clock we reached the house, where quite a company had gathered, eager and quiet, wondering what the foreign señorita might make of the situation, expecting that death would be the likely end of it all.

A sobbing, moaning heap by the fire proved to be a man of about twenty. He had broken the leg while riding a horse down one of those ravines. He howled when Doreen lifted the filthy cloth that covered the leg, but it was a simple fracture and he had actually pushed the bone into place himself. It did not look as though we could do more, at least by the light of the fire and flashlight, so Doreen gave him a shot of morphine and told his family we would stay until morning and see about him then. He went quickly to sleep, and we sat by the fire listening to the puffing, halting sounds of the *Tsahfihki* language. I had my notebook with me, as always, and jotted down a few words. Most of those in the house had come from a distance to see what would happen, and Doreen thought the talk would probably go on most of the night. She told our host we were tired, and he said that the upstairs platform was "ready." We took our ponchos and climbed the notched pole to a split palm platform that was bare except for a heap to one side that we took to be a person. I had not slept on the bare floor before without a pillow, but I slept and woke refreshed at dawn. The heap was a man, still sleeping soundly, but in another corner was a ragged green parrot who sat motionless with his eye fixed upon us. I fixed my eye on his until he felt it was time to get up. He walked cautiously down the pole from his perch, using his beak to pull himself along, and stepped daintily across the floor, his toes demurely pointed inward, until he reached a neat little package wrapped in banana leaves and tied with a vine. This he examined for some minutes, walking around and over it to judge it from all angles. Then he carefully opened it with claws and beak, eating the contents, which I could not identify but which seemed without doubt to be meant for his breakfast. Doreen and I went to the river, a lovely, clear-flowing stream, with smooth brown rocks on the bottom, to wash, and came back to the house, put a bamboo splint on the broken leg, wound it tightly, and then sat until the arrival of a man they called the subchief. He told folktales, surrounded by an attentive group of young men, and we listened, trying to learn and put down on paper some of what we heard. Soon a small boy shyly offered me a banana package, which I undid (was everyone's breakfast prepackaged, or was this a special service for parrots and visitors?) and found it contained four boiled eggs, several *asados*—not-quite-ripe plantains roasted to a delicious golden brown in the ashes, better than any hot roll I had ever tasted—and *bala*, the main staple of the Colorado diet, heavy, rubbery cylinders made of boiled, mashed, rolled green plantains. A few nuggets of dark brown rock salt were tucked into the packet. Doreen and I ate with great relish, keenly watched by every eye. There was a respectful silence until we finished eating, then the horses were saddled for us and we started, unaccompanied, for home.

The thirteen ravines which we had negotiated safely in the dark were far more frightening now. We could see in the daylight how steep was the pitch, how far down the river, how slick the mud. We plunged and rose, plunged and rose, clutching alternately at saddle and mane, and finally crossed the last of them. I wondered how the horses were to be returned to their owners, but a few minutes after we reached San Miguel, an Indian appeared, having come on foot and having timed his arrival exactly. As he mounted one of the horses and rode off into the forest, leading the other, I marveled. There was something so quiet and smooth about the way Indians did things. They knew how things needed to be done in the jungle, and without fuss or explanation they did them. But when we got home we were "in a flap," to use one of Doreen's expressions, having to unpack, to scrape the mud off our legs and bathe, to catch up with work undone, to talk and talk and talk about the night's events, describing for Dorothy and Barbara the awful ride and the bizarre sleeping quarters. But then it is quite likely, I suppose, that the Colorados were talking and talking about their bizarre visitors and their freakish ways.

"Did you see the way they climbed that pole?"

"Did you see how they ate?"

"They are so pale, they smell so strange, their teeth are so white, their lips so red," they were probably saying.

11

Distractions

We foreign women were anomalies in every way, but perhaps the thing that aroused more curiosity among our neighbors than anything else about us was that we seemed to have no men. Single women are subjected to rude questions everywhere, and our situation in San Miguel was as indefinable as it is anywhere. Many times we were asked if we were going to get married, were we married, did we not wish to be married? Then, as though in the mind of the questioner there was no connection with the previous questions, we would be asked how many children we had. No children? No, we were unmarried. But—not even *one child*? Poor señorita!

Only once did we have American tourists visit us, and they were two bachelors who wanted to "see the jungle." They accompanied me back from Quito, along with a single woman missionary named Edna who had been working in the city and wanted a taste of jungle life. It was certainly the full treatment for them. We rode from Santo Domingo to San Miguel in the heaviest rain I had ever been out in, so that we had to shout to make ourselves heard. I had had to lend my poncho to Edna, and my high boots were soon filled to the tops with water. Saddles, bridles, and reins were sodden, and I had to dismount repeatedly to adjust bridles and tighten cinches for these adventurers who were wishing with all their hearts that the adventure were a little more convenient. The men worried about getting muddied from head to toe, for although the horses could do no more than walk, pulling hoofs laboriously out of the sucking mud and plunging down in again, up to their bellies, the mud flew, painting us all a single color. They worried, too, about being bitten by gnats and mosquitoes, they worried about the water and the food when we finally reached the house in San Miguel. Was it safe? Might they get malaria? Parasites? Diarrhea? They might indeed, but so far as I know, they didn't. We thought we had done pretty well to turn out a meal of manioc root patties, jungle cabbage, plantain chips, lemonade, and caramel pie. Who could complain at that?

I took them all on a short walk to see a real Indian house, but it seemed a long walk to them, and they came back sore. The roof leaked over their beds. They left San Miguel sooner than they had planned, one of them with a poisonous ant bite, another with swollen ankles. Edna fell from her horse on the way to Santo Domingo and was dragged for a short distance in the mud. It rained all the way into town, and as I bid them good-by when they got on the banana truck for Quito, one of the men said he would be praying for the missionaries in a different way after that.

The people in the clearing had something to talk about for a few days. Which of the señoritas would be marrying the visitors? When? But gradually they accepted our explanation that the men had not come to propose to us, that the men had in fact let us know that it was not their intention ever to marry, and that we ourselves still expected to remain single.

It would have made our work easier if we could have put the whole matter out of mind. Three out of the four of us badly wished to be married. Only Barbara had given up the idea. She had been engaged before she left England, but when she was called to missionary life that ended it. She told me this much of her past history one afternoon as I sat on a fence while she, dressed in a rather filmy Sunday dress with blue flowers that matched her eyes, her legs caked with mud, hacked away with her machete at a rusted horse halter. She had loved the man, she said, and was afraid she still did. She would not dare to return to England. She might see him and the pull would be too great.

I wondered what the man would think if he could see her then—the blue dress, the mud, the flailing machete. Or later, when I watched her trying to support and drag a drunken Colorado from her front gate, after he had tumbled from his horse. The horse had started a fight with a stallion, and eight hoofs were flying as Barbara tried to get near enough to rescue the Indian. She got him to the house and laid him on a bench with a blanket over him while he bawled at the top of his lungs before falling into a stupor. In the morning he rode off, still in possession of the money he had made from selling his *achiote* in town. Someone would probably have relieved him of it had he not been so lucky as to fall

91

into Barbara's yard. Barbara, instead of soothing her own child's bruised knee as she might have been doing in some quiet English village, was here, bringing succor to a hard-drinking Indian for the love of Christ.

A young Ecuadorian named Abdón was interested in Doreen. She had gone through agonies of indecision for several years but nothing had been resolved. "Mixed" marriages—racially or religiously mixed—were generally frowned upon by the missionary community, and there were those who questioned the sincerity of the young man's conversion—wasn't it a typical Latin trick to land a wealthy foreigner and thus promote himself? Letters came in the mail for Doreen that were unsettling to her, chance encounters with her suitor or her critics upset her greatly, and there was endless talk.

Dorothy never tried to hide her eagerness to get married. She, too, had had her interests in the past, and now an Ecuadorian divorcé appeared on the scene, professing conversion to Protestantism and asking her to marry him. The same objections made to Doreen were made to Dorothy, with the added horror of the man's having been divorced. How could she consider it? Did she realize what she was doing? What if his first wife took it into her head to torment her, as some said an Ecuadorian woman might very well do? Then, too, the man was probably "involved" with women other than his ex-wife.

Letters from Jim kept coming to me, irregularly because of the great irregularity of mail service, but he wrote, and each time a letter came I opened it with trembling hands. Might he by now have decided that life alone in the jungle was not what he wanted after all? Certainly it was not what I wanted.

We were as distracted by all of this as single women in their twenties usually are, but at the same time we were striving with everything in our power to find a place for ourselves in the community, in the work we had to do, in our relationships, and in the will of God. The necessity of using two languages, Spanish and English, every day, and of having to study a third, brought sharply to our consciousness our alien status. Perhaps I should speak only for myself in this, for I felt it keenly. There was something marvelously haphazard about Dorothy. She breezed along. She learned plenty of Spanish words very quickly and strung them together in any way that suited her, making extraordinary constructions out of very ordinary ideas. She spoke fluently—that is, she poured out the words in an unhesitating stream, and it never bothered her very much to have people look at her blankly. She liked them all, and they knew it and liked her in return. I wasted much time myself in the effort to make sure the sentence would work before trying it out. Dorothy's method was more effective than mine in making friends, and it was making friends that mattered.

I spent many hours in meditation on the reasons we were here. It is a good thing to have a clear purpose and to go after it steadily, and while I knew God had called me to this job, I often felt restless and uncertain. When it came right down to spending the given hour on a hot, damp afternoon, if I had already worked for several hours on *Tsahfihki*, helped Doreen give a few injections or pills, written some letters, and read the Bible, I was often in a quandary. I would sit at the big table and doodle. Dorothy would be bustling cheerfully in the kitchen. She made things like wonderful little raisin tarts. This was a tedious task, since she could bake only two or three at a time in the round oven. She made stews and puddings and other things that tasted marvelous when we had been having rice, plantain, and beans for days. She was perfectly happy spending the better part of the day in the kitchen, and I envied her this carefreeness.

This was a part of the process of disentangling myself from the life I had known and giving myself completely to a new one. "No man that warreth entangleth himself with the affairs of this life, that he may please him who hath chosen him to be a soldier" were words written in my college yearbook by Jim Elliot. The daily insistent question was: Which were the affairs of this life? We had to eat. We had to live in reasonable cleanliness. We had to maintain some standards. Or were we wrong? What we ate, what we called clean, what standards we maintained, would have offended our neighbors here as well as our relatives back home—too good for the one group, too poor for the other. We were between two worlds, we were here by the grace of God, and we expected Him to give us light.

One of the recurring dreams was of going into a dime store. That became to me almost a dream of paradise—to be able to wander freely among the displays of vegetable parers and shining pots, dishcloths, notebooks, Scotch tape, nail files, the little ordinary things that made the difference between a civilized life and the life around us. We had some of these things, enough to make us the envy of Don Miguel's family, but they were always getting broken or rusty or mildewed, and the fact that they could not easily be replaced made me regard them as precious. The familiar became the stuff of dreams, and the stuff of former dreams—the jungle, Indians, thatched roofs, campfires, a strange unwritten tongue—became familiar.

Erik Erikson has said that maturity means maintaining continuity with the past in the presence of growth and change. It is a painful process. It was natural to feel that I must forsake all that I had known before in order to give myself wholly to the life of the people to whom God had called me. I strove consciously to embrace change instantly and completely, to be satisfied with the unfamiliar. I sometimes read the Bible in Spanish, and occasionally prayed in Spanish even when alone. But usually when I was alone, I felt that I could not do without some of the spiritual helps that meant most to me. It was only gradually that I came to understand that some things are meant to be cherished and not sacrificed. God was responsible for my parentage, my nationality, and my upbringing. He had called me, and He had called me by name, and He would not bypass what I was or the things that had made me what I was. If it had been ten or twenty years later, I would probably have wasted a great deal of time pondering things like "identity crisis" and "self-image." I did not know those terms then. As it was, I kept reading the Bible, usually in English, and I kept praying for wisdom, understanding, and growth in grace, and I found comfort in reading hymns over silently from a leather-bound copy of the *Keswick Hymnal* a friend had given me as a going-away present. I could hear them in my mind as I used to hear them sung, hymns like

> Guide me, O Thou Great Jehovah,
> Pilgrim through this barren land,

I am weak, but Thou art mighty,
Hold me with Thy powerful hand.

The singing of our little group of believers, that raucous, nasal bleating as they dragged their weary way through Spanish hymns, was satisfying to me only because it showed that there was faith in this far-off place. But it took the memory of strong, clear singing in English of great old hymns to fortify my soul.

12

Birth and Death

Night fell quickly in the jungle. This was partly because we were surrounded by tall trees, but twilight near the equator is brief; the night seems more literally to "fall," sometimes clear with a velvet sky perforated with stars, sometimes murky and black, a blackness that seems tangible. You know the sky is covered with clouds, but you can see nothing. You are closed in a silent depth as at the bottom of a deep lake.

There are also wild nights of tropical wind and rain when the forest roars around you and the swish and sweep of water falling on the roof, rushing into the gutters and rain barrels, and pouring in waterfalls as it overflows to the ground wakes you from sleep and sends you scurrying to weight down the papers on the desk or move things away from the windows which cannot be closed. You are reminded of the passage in the Book of Job about God's "tilting the water skins of heaven."

Each house in the clearing had its *lamparilla*, which on clear nights we could see gleaming in the windows until eight or nine o'clock when people went to bed. Not much reading was done in those houses and talk usually ran out by that time. Occasionally we could see the glow in kitchens where *fogóns* were left to smolder.

There were bats. They were vampire bats with hideous demonic faces, a fleshy horn, and two grotesque ears. In the daytime they hung themselves upside down under the thatch, or crawled inside the hollowed palm trunks that were the main support of our house, and we could hear their horrid squeaking. At night we felt the fanning of their wings as they swooped over our beds. There were fruit bats, too, once in a while, huge things with a wingspread of more than a foot, that would come after bananas if we left them unprotected in the kitchen. Since none of our walls reached the roof, there was nothing at all to keep the creatures out of our house.

It was on one of those blackest of jungle nights (perhaps I remember it as one of the blackest because it was a very dark night in other ways) that I was awakened by someone banging hard on the door downstairs. I was alone in the house, for Dorothy had gotten stranded in Quito because of an avalanche on the Santo Domingo road. I heard a man's voice, greatly agitated, calling, "Señorita, señorita!" I went to the top of the stairs and asked what the trouble was. His wife was giving birth and was about to die. I told him he ought to call the Señorita Barbara—she was a midwife.

He had called her, he said. She was on her way, but she had asked him to call me as well. I dressed quickly and took a flashlight, glad of the chance to help.

I had witnessed the birth of two babies. The first was a perfectly normal delivery by a woman in her twenties who had already had so many children she had lost count. Her husband, when he was sure we were on our way to help her, disappeared. The woman was sitting on the edge of a board bed, wearing a cotton dress. In no time a tiny creature was twisting its way into the world of the living, an awesome sight to me then and every time I've seen it since—the livid purple changed to healthy pink before your eyes, the black eyes popping open and looking at the new world, the choking cry, "I'm here." The second time we were called to a girl of eighteen having her third. Her man sat stolidly on the front porch, weaving a basket. The placenta was delayed, causing us much worry for a couple of hours, but at last it came, and everything was over. No one had made any fuss. The arrival of another living soul was not of great interest to anyone but the mother, quite an ordinary event to be got over without any to-do. They gave us cups of strong, sweet cocoa made with water, and we went home.

This time things were different. The man who called us was one of the Quiñones family, bitter enemies of the Evan-gélicos, and in whose house Carlota held her school. Two sons and their father lived in the house, apparently sharing one woman named Maruja. Barbara had delivered Maruja's last child, the tenth or twelfth, but there had been serious complications and Barbara and Doreen had both agreed that they could not take the responsibility for the next. They told the woman this clearly, urging her not to have any more children. When she became pregnant again, Doreen tried to impress upon her the danger she was in in order to persuade her to go to the hospital in Quito where she could be taken care of. Maruja said she understood the problem Doreen was describing, but since she had had so many children so easily, she went casually on about her business. One more would hardly matter. Doreen had then begged the men, first one and then another (not sure to whom the woman technically belonged), to take a serious view of the situation and get poor Maruja some help. They smoked their cigarettes and looked off across the clearing and said yes, they would certainly do exactly as Doreen had said, it was indeed a grave matter. When eight months had gone by and no move had been made, both Barbara and Doreen tried again. They went to the Quiñones men to repeat forcefully that neither would be able to help in the delivery. It would be beyond their skills. The men must get her to the hospital. Yes, indeed, they said, they would without fail take her mañana. But of course they had not, and now the woman was in desperate condition.

Barbara was just scraping the mud from her tennis shoes when I arrived. We were taken upstairs to an open porch that ran through from front to back in the center of the house, with rooms on either side. The oldest Quiñones, father of the other two, sat with his back to us near the railing, blowing smoke out into the mist of the night. We heard moaning and crying. One of the younger men took us into the room where the woman lay imploring God, the Blessed Virgin, and all the most holy saints to have mercy on her. There were pools of blood on the board bed, the ragged covers were stained as well. With all that blood around, I could not imagine that the baby was yet unborn, but I saw no signs of it until there was a small snuffling behind me, and I turned to find it lying on a pile of filthy rags on another bed. Someone had halfheartedly wrapped a rag around it and deposited it there where it could die in peace. The mother was throwing herself wildly from side to side on the bed so that Barbara could not examine her. The man suddenly fell into a paroxysm of crying and rushed out of the room.

"She's dying, she's dying!" he yelled, and Barbara saw that he was right—the woman had a prolapsed uterus. There were signs of shock so we elevated her feet and heated green plantains in the ashes of the fire to place around her like hot-water bottles. I tried unsuccessfully to find a pulse. She was weak from loss of blood but kept clawing the air, writhing and wailing, "I can't stand it, help me, I'm going out of my mind! O God! O holy Virgin! O most holy Virgin, have mercy! I'm dying!" The young man came back into the room at the sound of her cry and tried to calm her, but ended by joining her wails and rushing out again. Barbara saw that there was nothing we could do. The men would have to carry her immediately over the trail into Santo Domingo to the nuns' hospital. Perhaps she would survive the trip—jungle women had often proved to be unbelievably resistant to dying. The men stopped their howling and muttered between themselves. The woman's last child had died, and both men believed that Doreen had probably killed it. The Señorita Barbara would very likely end up killing Maruja herself this time, so perhaps it was best to take her to the nuns. They acted as though the thought had never occurred to them before, but they were soon fixing a blanket sling, fastened on a long pole, on which to carry her. The older man went off to find more men to help. I stayed with Maruja. She had quieted down, perhaps because of the medicine Barbara had given her, but perhaps, on the other hand, she was quiet because her strength was gone.

She began to speak and I leaned close to her. "Good-by," she was saying, "good-by to all my friends." Her voice gained strength and she spoke in a peculiarly oratorical tone. "Good-by to my family whom I have loved, good-by to my newborn child, my son, my little one, this child whom God has given and from whom He takes the mother. I commend him now into the arms of all of you. I am going crazy. I am out of my senses now, I must bid you all good-by."

I went to call Barbara, but she was still talking to the men. When I went back into the room, Maruja was making strange guttural noises. The young man came in and gave a howl. "She's already dead!" he shrieked and rushed from the room, sobbing and screaming. He began to claw the walls, literally trying to climb them. The father came back when he heard the cries, and there was no comforting either of them. They had forgotten we were there. I stood looking at the dead face, its jaw working back and forth and finally settling into a macabre grin. Neighbors began to come in. Someone took the baby, and Barbara and I went back to our respective houses in the early morning darkness. I tried to sleep, but the horror of the experience, the howls of the distraught men, and the hammering of coffin nails across the clearing kept me staring at the thatch above my head.

For the first time I had seen someone die. And I had seen the despair that death brought to the three men who surely had never learned to put their hope in God.

There was another reason for my sleeplessness that night and the restlessness of succeeding days. We had been defeated. An opportunity had been given us to reach the most resistant family in San Miguel, the Quiñones. It was a life-and-death matter, and if God had spared Maruja's life, the whole Quiñones tribe might have been delivered from spiritual death. In my heart I could not escape the thought that it was God who had failed. Surely He knew how much was at stake. Surely He could have done better by all of us. To my inner cries and questionings no answer came. There was no explaining any of it. I looked into the abyss . . . there was nothing there but darkness and silence.

13

Times and Seasons

About a week after Maruja's death the pitiful motherless baby was brought to Doreen for treatment. It was sick and thin as a skeleton and appeared to have syphilis. Doreen did what she could for it, but it was obviously not being loved and died a few days later. Its "two fathers" had fed it only water.

The effect on me of these deaths—a woman I had hardly seen before and a tiny scrap of an infant—would not have been so profound, I suppose, if we had had many distractions in our life in San Miguel. But life was a long, slow wait, with "world enough and time" for reflection, and I know now that that was what I needed. Missionary work, of all vocations, required a sinewy faith. Maruja's death produced a tremor in the foundations. If God had actually wanted us here at all, if we knew how to pray, if in fact He was concerned with the salvation of the Quiñones family, would He not have spared the mother and child? If Maruja or her men had had any glimmer of faith, if we had had any reason to believe that she had died in the peace of God, it would have made all the difference. As it was, the Quiñones household remained beyond our reach. We had not helped at all.

An excerpt from a letter I wrote to Jim will show what it was like:

> I find that I very soon get stale and fed up with life here. Contrary to your life, too busy and too full, mine is slow and eventless often, and the days drag by. It is spiritually enervating in a peculiar way. The quotation from Hudson Taylor on my China Inland Mission calendar is just the opposite of what I need now. "The intense activity of our times may lead to zeal in service, to neglect in personal communion; but such neglect will not only lessen the value of the service, but tend to incapacitate us for the higher service." I find that because nothing actually presses me to activity, I dawdle in quiet time, let my mind wander in prayer, and daydream when trying to study. Sometimes, I confess, after a long time on my knees and very little praying done (for the thousand trivialities that beckon my attention), I call it quits, saying to myself, "This isn't prayer. Might as well be up and *doing* something, even if it's only baking a cake or sharpening a pencil." . . . I feel that I have lost much since college days. It cannot be excused because I'm getting old or because the devil tempts me more now—the Lord has promised to "lead us in triumph."

My letters to Jim were often written over a period of days, for there was no mailbox to put them in. They sat on my desk until it happened that someone was going "out"—to

Quito or to Santo Domingo where ET would take them to Quito for us. Even in Quito there were no mailboxes at that time that could be trusted. Letters had to be taken directly to the post office and the stamps canceled if you wanted to be sure they would reach their destination. Otherwise, stamps were often stolen from the envelopes and letters were discarded. Still, it was a precarious business, for several times the bags in which our mail was being carried were stolen from the backs of trucks. Doreen had lost a suitcase that had been thrown on top of a banana cargo and, according to the conductor, had fallen off somewhere along the way. The suitcase had in it checks she had received from friends in England, her address book, clothes, a picture of her Ecuadorian suitor, and the mail that Dorothy, Barbara, and I had entrusted to her.

An Ecuadorian who was bringing mail for us from Quito had his luggage stolen. Only one who has been isolated as we were from all that tied us to our past can imagine what such a loss meant. When someone was going to town, we made out our lists with great care and anticipation. To be able to send letters was a pleasure, and the idea of receiving them was greater. With what eager straining and anticipation we waited for the return of the messenger. Sometimes he brought what we had asked for, sometimes he did not, for one reason or another. Sometimes he forgot. Sometimes he couldn't get things. Sometimes he was robbed. The apostle Paul knew such eventualities and could write, "All things are for your sakes." It was a very bitter pill to swallow. *All* things?

One day when Doreen arrived home from Quito, Barbara asked her if she had brought "fresh time." I took it that she meant "fresh thyme" and wondered how, in her simple cooking, she planned to use it. I learned that she wanted to set her watch. It was only when someone came "in" from "outside" that we had "fresh time."

There were things like avalanches, too. At times the road to Quito was cut off, and nothing came or went. Once, for a period of weeks, the railroad connecting Quito to the Pacific coast was interrupted by a landslide. This meant that no fuel was transported from the coast, which meant that no banana trucks ran to Santo Domingo, which meant that we got no mail and very few supplies. We had no gasoline for our pressure stoves or our lanterns. We cooked entirely on a *fogón* and used candles for light. We could not iron our clothes. We felt exiled and became more discouraged. A man came on horseback one day to encourage us. He said that it would be only fifteen more days before things would be coming through, and that they were building a bridge across the chasm created by the avalanche. When gasoline did at last begin to arrive, we had to pay eighty-four cents a gallon for it.

I missed the four distinct seasons of the year, which I had always known. They are among God's greatest gifts, each giving its own special delights and a respite from the others that enables us to appreciate them more fully. Each brings an opportunity for a fresh beginning, new activities. I loved closed curtains and an open fire, but we had no curtains, no windows to close, and only the smoking *fogón*. I loved open windows, warm air blowing in, but we often had cold air and wetness. I loved spring cleaning and putting away winter clothes, and I loved getting winter clothes out again. We had the same limp dresses and skirts week in and week out. I loved the quiet and isolation that bad weather brings, but we had more of this than we wanted. San Miguel was in the rain forest and had two seasons, a rainy one and a rainier one, though of course they were called "dry" and "rainy." The "dry" season meant light rain, a lot of mist, and cloudy weather. The rainy season was one of extremes—more sunlight and more rain than in the "dry," rain such as I had never imagined in the temperate climate of Pennsylvania and New Jersey, a million lances of water pouring straight down from the sky, turning the clearing into a dancing lake, setting a vast orchestra of frogs (where had they been till then?) to tuning. The next day there would be bright sunshine. It was "all or nothing at all" sort of weather, more interesting than endless days of gloom and halfhearted dampness.

To the jungle people, of course, there were other recognizable seasons, according to the flowering or fruit-bearing of certain trees or the harvest of corn and cotton. They paid no attention to clocks or calendars as we did, but we wanted to sharpen their recognition of certain occasions. Our first serious attempt to do this was a Christmas program planned for the schoolchildren and their parents that included the sort of songs and recitations we were used to, and that was to end with the giving of gifts.

Dorothy went to Quito to buy the gifts, and somehow managed to forget to bring them back with her. We were in despair. How could we make a Christmas for the children without them? This was to be our big occasion. The children did not know there were to be gifts and would not miss them, but to us it was unthinkable. There was nothing for it but that one of us go up and get the toys that Dorothy had packed carefully and left in our *bodega*, or storeroom. I was the one to go. The trips to Quito were always major undertakings—the horseback ride to Santo Domingo that might take two hours or four, depending on the state of the mud; the night spent in town on the cot at ET's house, or, if I could arrange it, in somebody's *bodega*, with an ear cocked for the sound of the trucks starting up early in the morning (on this occasion I had been told that they would leave at five, but at four-thirty I heard them actually pulling out of the plaza. I sprang from the cot, dressed, and rushed out to find the plaza dark and quiet, the last truck apparently having left. No, there was one, with a single seat left, and they let me on); the long, grinding journey up through the mountain pass from heat to wind and cold and drizzle; the people jammed together on the narrow board seats with narrow board backs, chickens and pineapples hanging over the windows, children held out the windows from time to time since there are no "rest stops" at all; long waits in little towns where someone's sister-in-law has been promised a ride but she is not quite finished with her breakfast when the truck arrives; long waits on the road, far from any dwelling, for reasons that are neither explained nor inquired about; a long wait at the chain, long waits at tiny coffeehouses; and long, long, slow pulls in first or second gear, up and up into the mist until at last, through a break in the clouds, you see the green paradise of Quito's valleys spread below and you begin the groaning, jerking descent to the Inter-Andean Plain. (This time I thought of Jim—was there the slightest chance that he would be in Quito for Christmas?) At last the city, the cobblestones, the narrow streets with radios screeching and children scurrying in front of the truck; finally, the crowded, teeming station where the bananas are unloaded and the passengers climb down from their perches and collect their baskets and burlap sacks and chickens and crates of *maranjillas*—a small orange fruit, the size of a golfball, which has pulp like a green tomato and tastes like a strawberry. For a traveling missionary like me there would be another missionary's house, a hot bath, the bliss of civilized clothes and food, rugs on the floor, polished furniture, people who spoke English, then taxis, buses, exchanging money, and shopping. (Jim was not there, there wasn't even a letter. If he had known I would be there, would he have come? I did not know.) Another banana truck back again to the jungle, another night in a *bodega*, another horseback ride, a bath in the river, and I would be home. But this time I reached home too late for the Christmas program. The truck broke down and there was a twenty-four-hour delay. "Mañana, señorita. What is a day? Mañana the truck will go." The whole trip for nothing? Would the others have the program without the gifts? They did. I arrived home on Christmas Eve, a few hours after the program had been held.

On Christmas morning I was awakened by little Vicente coming into my room, waving a British flag and singing "God Save the Queen" in English. Tropical foliage outside my window, no snow, no evergreens; I was in Ecuador, not the States. There was no tree to be lighted, there were no presents to be opened by us. But we did get around to singing a few carols with our little pump organ, and we had a feast for dinner: chicken with all the fixings, which in this case were manioc root, carrots, squash, mashed green plantains, coleslaw, coffee, and an English suet pudding with hard sauce, the gift of another missionary.

14

The Life around Us

Most people think of the jungle as a place crawling with snakes and all sorts of other noxious creatures. It is. If you are a jittery person, you have to learn to function without worrying too much about what might drop on your head or hide in your shoe or creep up your leg at any moment. If you are not by nature jittery, you must learn a healthy respect for snakes and things, because they are there, and you will have to watch for them. I began to develop the habit of sorting with my eyes the sticks and leaves as I walked along the trail—some of them might turn out to be snakes or *congas*, a very large ant whose bite was said to be as painful as that of a snake but not lethal. I felt a *conga* crawling on my neck once but managed to flick it off before it had a chance to attack. The cockroaches that lived in our kitchen walls were so huge we could actually hear them walking around at night. One dropped onto my bed, and when I turned on my flashlight to identify the visitor I was astonished at its size. Surely it was three inches long. Cockroaches became to me the most revolting of all vermin. They laid great long strings of eggs in our cupboards and clothes boxes. They came out of the walls by the dozens at night and foraged for food in the kitchen cupboards, crawling into our pots and pans, freshly washed dishes and silverware, swarming over tables and counters and leaving their filth behind. If you stepped on one, you might be sickened to see a long, wiry worm loop its way out.

I discovered one morning that the backs of my thighs were covered with what looked like insect bites. Closer examination revealed a tiny vermin clinging to each red swelling. I went to Doreen, and she took one look and screamed, "Oh, kid, do you know what you've *got*?" I said I didn't, and spitting out the *s* and the *c* as only the British can do, she said "*Scabies*!" It sounded awful. It sounded like a cross between scurvy and rabies. It wasn't that serious, Doreen assured me, it was only a mite that burrows into your skin and lays its eggs, but I didn't like the sound of that. Usually it affects people who live in filth, so I set about a great washing, bathing, scrubbing, and cleaning the house, the outhouse, and myself. Doreen gave me something to rub on the bites after I had got the mites off with a brush, and in a day or so I was free of them. Later I was visited at different times by sand fleas which burrow under the toenails and lay eggs, by lice, and by chiggers, which are particularly fond of burrowing into the flesh around your belt line.

There were both snakes and scorpions around, but I had no narrow escapes myself with either of these when I lived in San Miguel. We did occasionally have to treat others who had been bitten.

There were also many delightful creatures. On my way to Soledad's house one day I saw an insect that while flying looked like a brilliant vermillion helicopter, but upon landing looked like nothing but a black speck, and there was a bumblebee nearly four inches long that would zoom up from the pathway with a buzz like a distant bomber. It was one of my sorrows that I never found a book on jungle flora and fauna in English. I wanted very much to learn the names of these fascinating things.

The streams were full of small fish called *campeches*. They were armored rather than scaled, and were shaped like triangular prisms, with a very broad mouth. It was their habit to hide under rocks, and if you knew how to do it, you could catch them with your hands. It was comical to watch a group of Indian children, whooping and shrieking, trying to grab the *campeches*' tails between their second and third finger as they reached around a rock, lying nearly on their faces in the water. The fish would often get away and go leaping and sailing downstream, the children leaping and yelling after them. It was in order to catch these fish, Soledad later explained to me, that the Indians blackened their hands. They would be less visible in water.

There were beautiful ocelots in the forest, though I saw only their skins as the Colorados took them to sell in town. A child once took me to a tree that he said he had just seen an ocelot climb. I clambered over some fallen banana trees and through some dense brush, hoping to catch a glimpse of that spotted coat, but it disappeared and all I got for my

pains was a large pod of breadfruit that had fallen nearby.
We cooked and mashed it for supper to eat in place of the
usual plantains, but decided we liked plantains better.

The birds were almost as elusive as the wild animals. There
were parakeets, macaws, toucans, and probably a hundred
other varieties less easily identifiable, but rarely did they perch
in trees where we could see them. They kept to themselves in
the forest, seldom even flying across the open spaces. But we
heard their twittering and trumpeting and screeching, and
sometimes Vicente would help us to see them. On a walk
in the woods he would stop dead and listen when we had
heard nothing, and then exclaim in delight, "Look, a pretty,
precious little bird!" My father had been an amateur orni-
thologist, able to imitate with near-perfect accuracy the calls
of about sixty birds, and he had often taken us children on
"bird walks." I learned then the necessity of being trained to
see birds. To the untrained eye, they did not seem to be there.

In later years, as I learned to know the Indians better, I
realized how unusual it was for Vicente to have appreciated
the beauty of a bird. Not many Indians seemed to be aware
of the loveliness around them. They noticed things that were
of some use to them: trees because the wood was useful,
or because they bore dyes, medicinal bark, silk cotton, or
fruit; birds because they were edible; rocks because you could
sharpen a machete or grind corn with them. A mountain,
a river, an orchid, or a sunset they took quite for granted.
"That mountain, señora? Why, it's been there." "The sunset?
The sun always goes down."

I began to think, when I lived in the jungle, of the harmony of God's universe. I could see His love in creating

a hummingbird with flashing color and dainty wings. The power of the divine imagination—so stunningly displayed to Job in the descriptions of dawn and darkness, hoarfrost and thunderbolt, wild goats, asses, oxen, and ostriches, and those awesome beasts Behemoth and Leviathan—that power seemed present to me in the great silence of the forest and in the tropical storms, in the design of the "helicopter" insect, in the piping of the tree toads—what kind of imagination did it require to bring such wonders into being? My mind soared, trying to comprehend it all, and I found it easy to worship the God who showed Himself in these things. But were the poisonous snakes and the vampire bats, the cockroach worms and the scorpions, also necessary to the world's harmony? That question took me back to the beginnings of things, to the great Unanswerable: Was sin necessary? Could men have lived in a world without suffering?

I did not know the answer then. I do not know it now. But I think during the first eventful year as a jungle missionary I had my first inkling that it is not a tidy world we live in. It is not a world we can deal with sentimentally. The God of the "pretty, precious little bird" is the God of that fierce creature "whose sneezings flash forth light," "whose heart is hard as stone."

But I was learning, too, in what I saw around me, in the life of the forest, and what I found within me of hope, disappointments, and confusions, that underneath are the Everlasting Arms.

15

A Fishing Expedition

Soledad asked for a few days off because a group of Indians was going fishing. We could come too, she said, if we liked. Any chance to be with the Indians and hear the language, I seized, and I told her we would come. She gave us directions to reach the spot where everyone was to meet: "Just down this trail, keep going straight until you come to some houses. About three hours. Tomorrow at sundown we will all be there."

Barbara and I left at one o'clock the next afternoon, taking with us Banco, Barbara's old white horse, loaded with my saddlebags, Barbara's saddlebags, and Vicente. I carried a little red lantern and a pot of soup in one hand, a machete in the other. Barbara led the horse.

We walked all afternoon. Past the familiar landmarks, past Colorado trails we knew, past the last banana plantation, beyond the wide, well-traveled trail to where it narrowed more and more as we went on. We met a woman who was amazed when we told her where we were going. "It's very, very far," she told us, and my heart sank, for I knew that the Indians considered five miles a short walk. What would a long one be? We came to a fork. Soledad had said, "Keep going straight." There was no way to do that. One or two clues led us to think that one trail led to an Indian house, so we took that, hoping to spend the night there, and perhaps learn the way to the rendezvous point. Seven dogs exploded from the house when we reached the clearing, followed by a shy girl, well painted, dressed in a colored striped skirt, hair uncombed but teeth well blackened. She understood almost no Spanish, and we could not make her understand that we were lost and needed directions. Finally, her father arrived— more paint, less clothing, blacker teeth, and better Spanish. When we tried six or seven ways of asking our questions, he assured us that we were on the right trail and would certainly reach our destination before nightfall—at six, he said, and I was not sure whether he meant at six o'clock that evening or six hours from then (it was about half past four). Again I explained to him that we meant today before the sun went down, not tomorrow, and he smiled and nodded enthusiastically, "*Si, si, si, si.*" So we thanked him, which he did not understand at all, and set off once more.

Vicente was a jungle encyclopedia. At every turn he would be pointing out something, telling us to catch something, to pick this leaf or that stick, to look at this bird or that insect, to listen to the toad's peeping. We found an odd arrangement of bamboo poles, and he explained that it was put there to catch water. Later he told us to collect some white sap that smelled of peppermint because it would start a fire. We found that he was right. Insects on the path that we had not seen at all he had noticed from high up on the horse, and warned us about. When the path seemed to peter out altogether, he found it for us, although he had never traveled this way before.

The three of us took turns riding the horse, and while I was riding, barefooted, because we had been crossing rivers, my foot suddenly began to burn as if a thorn branch had cut across my toes. I paid no attention to it until later in the evening, when I found that the foot was red and swollen, not scratched, and Vicente told me that a caterpillar had stung me.

The jungle became thicker and taller as we went, and darker as the sun sank, so that we were finally using a flashlight to watch for snakes and to find the trail. There were occasional hoofmarks to reassure us that the Indians had ridden this way before. We hoped they were the same Indians we were looking for and not others. Knowing how easy it was to lose the way in daylight, we began to think it would be madness to continue in the dark, but each bend of the trail gave us hope that we would come upon the clearing we were looking for. It got darker, the trail got more indistinct, and we got tired. The jungle was filled with night noises. We had long since left behind us the last habitation when we came to a place where it was impossible to tell which way the trail went, and we knew that the only rational thing to do was to stop. Vicente seemed terrified but could only tell us in *Tsahfihki* what it was he feared. Our *Tsahfihki* vocabulary stopped short of whatever it was that he was telling us.

We tied up the horse, lit the little red lantern, spread my nylon poncho on the wet floor of the forest, and spent nearly forty minutes starting a fire, for all the available wood was not only wet but rotten. We poured on kerosene and the white sap we had gathered, threw on armloads of palm fronds, and were at last able to drink hot soup from the pot I had been carrying. Vicente wanted to build a sleeping hut, which he no doubt could have done well, but neither Barbara nor I had the energy to chop the sticks he needed. We were exhausted from getting firewood with a blunt machete, the moon was bright and a hut did not seem nearly so important as it later turned out to be.

We all lay down on the poncho and spread Barbara's blanket over us. There were no mosquitoes, the moon shone beautifully through the trees, and we were thankful it was not raining. Suddenly out of the silence Barbara said, "Oh, I say, you know, there are all sorts of *huge* snakes around here."

"Do you see any?" I asked.

"No, but I'm sure they're about."

I knew they were, and we tried for a while to keep the fire going but ran out of wood and settled for keeping the burning lantern hung up on a tree. I slept a little but was awakened by Barbara's soft English voice again out of the dark, "Oh, I say, it's beginning to rain." Big drops were hitting hard on the wide heavy leaves around us, and soon were making so much noise we had to shout to hear one another. We got up and covered what we could of our things (my linguistic materials were safe in my cowhide saddlebag), then changed the blanket and poncho around, blanket on the ground, the waterproof poncho over us, and slept again. We were awakened

122

again by Vicente's laughter. He lay between us, giggling and choking with laughter.

"Whatever is so funny?" Barbara asked.

He had found himself lying in a lake of water which had come through the hole in the center of the poncho. We hadn't thought of that, but there was nothing to do about it.

I lay with my head under the poncho, feeling the rain on it, thinking about the spoor of a jaguar that I had seen on the way, and of the wild boars the Indians had told us of shooting. I kept hearing unidentified noises, some of which turned out to be our horse moving on his tether, champing leaves, blowing. I was not afraid of anything, but I didn't want to miss anything either.

Finally the dawn came and with it the cessation of the rain. We crawled out, stiff from trying to lie in one position so as not to disturb the puddles on top of the poncho. We had a bit of chocolate for breakfast and some squashed bread, and talked of whether to continue or to go back home. We decided to go on, for a couple of hours at least, sure that Soledad and company would be somewhere to be found. We blazed a trail with the machete to be sure we would be able to retrace our steps, and when after two hours we had found nothing encouraging, and knew that the journey home would take us about nine hours, we stopped in a tiny abandoned shelter next to a stream—the first water we had found since the previous day. We washed our grimy faces and muddy feet, made a fire and boiled water for tea. We had no separate pot for brewing so we dropped the tea leaves into the water, which also had in it ashes, palm splinters, and a spider. While we were resting and enjoying the tea, Blanco decided to go home. Without any warning, the horse crashed across the stream and plunged down the trail. Barbara sprinted after him. It did not occur to me that she would have difficulty in catching him, but I did not know Blanco. When he had made up his mind that he had had enough, it was his custom to go home. Half an hour passed without a sign of them. There we were, Vicente and I, with the lantern, the pot, the machete, the saddlebags, the blanket, and the poncho. (We had unloaded Blanco in order to give him a rest. He went off carrying only the saddle.) We shouted for Barbara, but got no reply. We waited, listening, but heard only the wind sighing in the trees. We shouted some more, but our voices were lost in the forest. The jungle suddenly became a place of great emptiness and vastness, even a hostile place. The Indians, who had so badly let us down, seemed malicious. Even Blanco was in league with malevolent forces. What were we to do now? There was nothing to do but load the stuff on our back and start walking. I don't know how long we walked before Vicente began to sob. He was tired, he said, he had been stubbing his toes and stepping on thorns, and he did not know where the Señorita Barbara was. I tried to cheer him, and he managed to keep going a little longer, muffling his sobs and stumbling and muttering about "those Indians and that no-good horse." All at once we saw Barbara coming toward us, riding Blanco. He had kept a few inches ahead of her, she told us, until he felt he had proved his point, when he at last allowed her to grab the bridle.

We were glad we had blazed a trail, for that part of the way took us less time than it had that morning. About two o'clock we came across a Colorado, standing alone in the forest. He greeted us and informed us that Soledad and her crowd had decided not to go fishing after all. It was as if he were there by appointment. How in heaven's name had he known where to find us? Why had he decided to find us at all? Now, nearly twenty-four hours later than agreed? No explanation was offered except that he had been out hunting *bravos*, the name given to wild boars, and he now seemed to be waiting for us to follow him.

He stepped lightly and quickly along the trail in front of us, a tall, muscular man, handsome in his paint, and straight as an arrow, his gun over one shoulder, a powder pouch over the other. We had a hard time keeping up and dragging Blanco along. The Indian stayed far enough ahead so that he might have a chance at shooting game. Once when he was out of sight altogether, we came to a fork. I thought of Paul and Silas, delivered from prison by an angel who took them to a "certain street" and then vanished. But almost as soon as we paused, we heard a peculiar shout. He had known that we would be baffled at that point and was waiting just beyond.

At last we reached our clearing, and by six o'clock we were bathing in the San Miguel River.

I never went into the jungle again on unknown trails without a guide.

16

A Fish or a Scorpion

One morning in January 1953 I was in my bedroom reading the *Daily Light*, a book of Scripture verses put together for each day of the year. The passage for that day (the twenty-sixth) was from 1 Peter, "Think it not strange concerning the fiery trial which is to try you, as though some strange thing happened unto you: but rejoice, inasmuch as ye are partakers of Christ's sufferings" (1 Pet. 4:12–13 KJV). Just as I finished reading those words, I heard gunshots. This was nothing unusual—Colorados and white men often hunted in the vicinity, so I took no particular notice. A few minutes later, however, it seemed that the whole *plaza*, usually such a tranquil, sleepy place, came awake all at once and I heard shouting and the thud of horses' hoofs and the sound of people running. Doreen's voice came, shrill and excited, over the din: "They've killed Don Macario!"

I ran out and heard the news repeated over and over: "Macario has been shot!" "Macario is murdered!" Don Lorenzo, one of the believers, had been with him. His story was disconnected, but as he told it, gasping for breath and starting from the beginning again and again, we understood that they had been clearing some brush to plant banana trees when some of the Quiñones family arrived and began to argue over the ownership of the land. Macario and Lorenzo said it belonged to Macario, and someone shot him. The body was there, Lorenzo said, just where it fell, only a short distance from the *plaza*.

"I'm going straight out there," Doreen said.

"Oh, no you're not," I said. "Don't do a thing until we get the authorities."

But there was no talking Doreen out of something she had made up her mind to do. She went, and in a short time she was back with four men who were carrying the body between them in a blanket. They laid it on the porch of Barbara's house, and the whole town hurried over for a look. Mothers brought their children, everyone stood wide-eyed and solemn in the presence of this awesome thing. Every corpse, said George MacDonald, looks as though it were the only one that had ever been. We gazed in silence for a long time. There was a great hole in Macario's forehead—he had been shot point-blank, Lorenzo said. Rigor mortis had set in, and one arm stuck up stiffly from the side, an accusing forefinger pointing off into space. The bluebottle flies had already found the corpse and laid their eggs in its hair. Flies crawled around the wound, around the slightly opened mouth and eyes.

We heard horses' hoofs on the other side of the clearing and turned to see Carlota, the schoolteacher, galloping toward the road for town, her cape flying in the wind.

"To inform the authorities she goes!" somebody said, and we realized it was a good thing someone had thought of it.

It would take several hours before anyone could possibly come from town, and there seemed to be nothing to do until then. Once they got used to the sight of Macario, gray in the face, stiffened, and with that gaping cave in his temple, the crowd began to talk. There had been a fight in the saloon the night before, someone said, and one of the Quiñones men had disputed Macario's right to some land on which he had planted bananas. Most of this jungle was frontier land, and a man who cultivated it, owned it, but the government was gradually taking control and requiring that claims be filed, and often the ownership was an open question. Until official recognition by title papers, settlements were frequently made informally, by fist- or gunfights.

It was not the Quiñones who had really done it, said some, it was the Quiñones' peon who had actually shot Macario. Perhaps he had been paid to do it. Wasn't Carlota angry because of the way the Evangélicos had treated her? Was it not she who had ridden into town before anyone else had thought of it? Had she known about it in advance? The Quiñones group had disappeared, of course, and no one knew for certain what the motive was.

In midafternoon two men from the sheriff's office arrived and declared that no prosecution could be made unless there was an autopsy. There was no doctor available, so a missionary named Bill who had come in with the authorities said he would give it a try. The bullets had to be gotten out, they said, for evidence in the trial, and this looked like a fairly straightforward sort of job, since it was clear where the bullets had gone in.

Doreen, always at her best in a crisis, rushed to her house and was soon back dressed in white (as she had been taught at the London Missionary School of Medicine)—white dress, white sandals and socks, even a white band around her unruly hair. In her hand she carried a meat saw. Bill was on his knees beside the corpse, probing directly into the cavern in the head while the crowd hovered close, shutting out light and air. It wouldn't do, the official said. You couldn't simply probe. The head would have to be "opened," as Doreen guessed. So Bill went to work with the saw, trying to slice open the skull. He had no idea of what he was in for, and was soon sawing away with all the strength and energy he possessed. People who had lost interest earlier came back, mothers called their children from play to come and watch, and a great shout went up, when, quite unexpectedly, the head, which had been cracked by the blast of the bullet, fell into several pieces. This was quite enough for most of the spectators, and when Bill had shown them a single fragment of lead, they began to disperse. Bill was in a lather from the exertion, Doreen was standing coolly by with adhesive tape, a basin, some towels, and forceps. The job could not be finished up neatly, but she and Bill did their best to put things back together. Macario would have to wear a turban, fashioned of a towel, into his grave.

When the autopsy was completed, it occurred to the two officials that something ought to be done about the murderers.

The people had, of course, reported who they were, but no one knew where they were, and since night was beginning to fall, the two men hurried out to the scene of the crime with flashlights. They poked around the underbrush for a time, and soon they were back with the report that no murderers were anywhere to be found. No, there were no murderers. Gone. That was that. So their horses were saddled up and they rode back to town, their duty done.

It was customary to have a wake when anyone died. The body must be "accompanied" during the night—first because no one would think of leaving a friend alone, then, very practically, because rats and cockroaches must be kept off. The wake gave people an opportunity to express, in an accepted form and manner, feelings that they would not otherwise know how to deal with. It was a catharsis for all concerned. Macario, however, had no home and no family nearby, so the Christians of the evangelical group held the wake in the school-and-meeting room. I went for a part of the time and joined in the hymn singing and coffee drinking. There were long periods of silence, also, and periods of praying. The air in the room was heavy, for by midnight the corpse was sixteen hours old. A single lamp glowed faintly, casting enormous shadows on the walls and ceiling of the schoolroom. The soles of Macario's bare feet, upright at the end of the table where they had laid him out, were very dark yellow. Still the rigid finger pointed.

Across the clearing we could hear hammering. The coffin was being nailed together.

In the morning they put shoes and socks on the cold feet and placed the body in the tapered box. Then we had a funeral service—hymns and prayers, a few halting words about our brother and his hope of the resurrection. When the service was over, the shoes were taken off. They were too valuable to be put in the ground with an already very ripe corpse. They would be given to his sister when she came from the coast to collect his few possessions. The lid was nailed into place and the coffin was carried on the shoulders of the men of the church, along the muddy trail, through the rain, to the Colorado cemetery. A few of the Indians who had been his friends were there, and one of them asked about tying a red thread. It was a Colorado custom when anyone died to tie a red thread around the finger of the corpse. The other end of the thread was held until the grave was filled in, and then it was tied to a stick which was stuck upright in the ground. After a week or so they would pull the thread, and if it came loose they would know that the soul had left the body. A Colorado would not be buried in a coffin. The lid had been nailed on Macario's coffin now, and after some discussion it was decided that there was no proper way to tie the thread. They would just have to trust that the soul would find its way out at the proper time. A roof of palm leaves was put up over the grave. One of the Christian men read a passage of Scripture, another prayed, and everyone went home again very slowly in the rain.

The events of the preceding day stayed vividly in my mind for a long time. It had been, I wrote to my parents, "the most nightmarish day of my life." As we walked home in the rain from the graveyard, it seemed to me that everything was over. Although I could, by no stretch of the imagination, hold myself responsible for Macario's murder, the enormity of it weighed me down almost as heavily as if I were guilty. It was another failure, somehow, a judgment on us and our work. I went over and over in my mind how it had come to be that I was here at all, that Macario had been my colleague. The work we did together was the work to which each had been clearly called. We had been called, had we not? I went back to the night in New Jersey when I had knelt in my room, asking for assurance that the call was God's voice and not a figment of my own mind. It had seemed that He answered me through a Bible verse, "I the Lord have called thee and will hold thine hand." I thought of those who had prayed for me and encouraged me in so many ways, I thought of all the sermons I had cringed under about the coldness of the churches and their disobedience to Christ's commission, "Go ye." I thought of all the times I had sung "Where He Leads Me, I Will Follow," earnestly examining my soul for signs of insincerity or impurity of motive. I could not deny the reality of that call or the faithfulness of those who had supported me. What of the work of Colorado translation? Could I possibly doubt that this was God's work? Was He, in fact, interested in the salvation of this jungle tribe, or was it only we three foreign women who were interested? Had I come here, leaving so much behind, on a fool's errand? If this was how the Lord of Hosts looked after His servants and His glory, if this was a sample of how He answered prayer for His work and His workers, it certainly fit none of my categories. How was I to reconcile His permitting such a thing with my own understanding of the missionary task?

Maruja's death had, of course, been a crisis that brought serious questions to the fore. But Maruja had not been a part of our program. Macario was God's answer to prayer, he was the key to the whole of the language work, he was (God knew) the only man on earth who spoke both Spanish and Colorado with equal ease. The work now came to a sudden full stop.

Doreen, Barbara, and Dorothy each had their own work, which was not directly affected by Macario's death. I was alone in my loss, and probably felt it more intensely because of the added sense of isolation. I could do nothing, be nothing. Without an informant, I was not a "linguist" or a translator. I could only wait.

As I look back on that time, I think it was Lesson One for me in the school of faith. That is, it was my first experience of having to bow down before that which I could not possibly explain. Usually we need not bow. We can simply ignore the unexplainable because we have other things to occupy our minds. We sweep it under the rug. We evade the questions.

Faith's most severe tests come not when we see nothing but when we see a stunning array of evidence that seems to prove our faith vain. If God were God, if He were omnipotent, if He had cared, would this have happened? Is this that I face now the ratification of my calling, the reward of obedience? One turns in disbelief again from the circumstances and looks into the abyss. But in the abyss there is only blackness, no glimmer of light, no answering echo.

When I was sixteen years old, I copied in the back of my Bible a prayer of Betty Scott Stam's, whose visit in our home when I was very small had made such a deep impression on me. Her prayer:

Lord, I give up all my own plans and purposes, all my own desires and hopes, and accept thy will for my life. I give myself, my life, my all, utterly to thee to be thine forever. Fill me and seal me with thy Holy Spirit, use me as thou wilt, send me where thou wilt, work out thy whole will in my life at any cost, now and forever.

The cost, for her, was quite literally her life only a few years after she had prayed that prayer. I had never forgotten the picture on the front page of our newspaper of the Stams' baby daughter being carried in a rice basket by a Chinese woman who had found her after her parents' execution.

I went back to things like that prayer as I searched for meaning to Macario's death. Only God knew Macario's heart, and whether he was a martyr. For me there were other implications. I had promised to obey God, and I had known that that promise might lead to "tribulation." I had prayed also for holiness, but this—this kind of "answer"—was startling and repugnant to me. I had desired God Himself and He had not only not given me what I asked for, He had snatched away what I had. I came to nothing, to emptiness.

Doreen took the poncho on which the autopsy had been performed and spread it over the fence between our two houses, in hopes that the rain would wash off the great splotch of blood in the middle of it, but it stayed there for weeks. Each time I saw it, I thought of the sight of those spilled brains, the only brains in the world that contained the languages I needed.

I felt like a son who had asked for a fish and been given a scorpion. I had honestly (surely it was honestly?) desired

135

God. I wanted to do His will. That bloody poncho mocked me.

It was a long time before I came to the realization that it is in our acceptance of what is given that God gives Himself. Even the Son of God had to learn obedience by the things that He suffered. He had come for only one purpose: "Lo, I come (in the volume of the book it is written of me,) to do thy will, O God" (Heb. 10:7 KJV). And His reward was desolation, crucifixion.

Amy Carmichael wrote:

> But these strange ashes, Lord, this nothingness,
> This baffling sense of loss?
> Son, was the anguish of my stripping less
> Upon the torturing cross?

Each separate experience of individual stripping we may learn to accept as a fragment of the suffering Christ bore when He took it all. "Surely he hath borne our griefs, and carried our sorrows" (Isa. 53:4 KJV). This grief, this sorrow, this total loss that empties my hands and breaks my heart, I may, if I will, accept, and by accepting it, I find in my hands something to offer. And so I give it back to Him, who in mysterious exchange gives Himself to me.

> Was I not brought into the dust of death,
> A worm and no man, I;
> Yea, turned to ashes by the vehement breath
> Of fire, on Calvary?
>
> O Son beloved, this is thy heart's desire:
> This, and no other thing

Follows the fall of the Consuming Fire
On the burnt offering.

Go on and taste the joy set high, afar—
No joy like that to thee;
See how it lights the way like some great star.
Come now, and follow Me.

17

My Wellbeloved's Leisure

The exchange of letters between Jim and me during the months I had been with the Colorados had not been frequent, but I detected a certain rise in temperature. Had Jim by now decided that marriage might facilitate rather than impede his missionary work? I could not help hoping, but I kept my letters as cool as I could.

Doreen had also kept up her correspondence with the young Ecuadorian, and it looked as though an engagement was not far off. Dorothy was visited from time to time by the Ecuadorian who was professing conversion and wanted her to marry him. Barbara was as detached as ever from all such extracurricular activities.

On the night of January 29, 1953, only three days after Macario's death, I was sitting as usual over my language notes when I heard the sound of horses' hoofs. I took the lantern outside and was greeted by a friend from Santo

Domingo who handed me a telegram. Jim was waiting for
me in Quito.

The ten-hour climb up the western slope of the Andes
by banana truck the next day had never seemed so inter-
minable. Never were there so many passengers to wait for,
never so many landslides to be cleared before we could pro-
ceed, never such a long delay at the chain. At last we came
over the top at San Juan and descended into the beautiful
valley where the city lay. There was a taxi ride from the
truck stop to the home of friends where Jim was staying, a
controlled greeting in the presence of others, dinner with
the others, and at long last an evening alone when he asked
me to marry him.

Before I gave him my answer I thought of a lot of things
he had said in the past about why he could not ask me to
marry him. I thought of what he had written in my college
yearbook, knowing that "the affairs of this life," from which
he intended to keep himself disentangled, included marriage.
I remembered his desire to be like the apostle Paul, free to
give himself to the work of the gospel without the hindrances
of wife and children, and I knew that his father had prayed
for this kind of life for Jim. I thought of an older missionary's warning that the Quichua work could not be done as
it ought to be done except by single men.

But I loved him. I had loved him for a long, long time and
I had tried to keep that love in a tight rein, praying often in
Amy Carmichael's words:

> And shall I pray thee change thy will, Father,
> Until it be according unto mine?

But no, Lord, no, that never shall be, rather
I pray thee blend my human will with thine.

I pray thee hush the hurrying, eager longing,
I pray thee soothe the pangs of keen desire,
See in my quiet places wishes thronging,
Forbid them, Lord, purge, though it be with fire.

And work in me to will and do thy pleasure,
Let all within me, peaceful, reconciled,
Tarry content my Wellbeloved's leisure,
At last, at last even as a weaned child.

And so I asked Jim if he believed God had given His permission for us to marry. He did, and that was enough for me.

But, he said, it might be five years or so before we could marry. Surely not, I thought, but I did not say it. Surely God would not ask us to wait another five years—we had waited five already since our first recognition of love. Jim explained that he had made commitments to do a lot of building for other missionaries. They came first. He wanted to do some itinerating throughout the Quichua territory before settling down. And there was one more thing.

"You must learn Quichua," he said.

"Before we get married?"

"Before we get married. I've seen enough of missionary wives who come out all starry-eyed, expecting to work alongside their husbands, and then get bogged down taking care of a household and having babies so that they never get around to learning the language. That won't happen to you. You'll learn it first."

I accepted the proposal and the conditions, willing to pay any price for this man, and that took care of the business for the evening. The rest of our time was spent in front of the fire, trying to express what we had never before been free to express.

I have told elsewhere* how what appeared to be an active case of tuberculosis was discovered when I had a routine chest X-ray shortly after our engagement. Further tests showed it was a mistake, or as Jim suspected, perhaps God had healed me in the interim, in answer to prayer, but our confidence in God's leading was for several days sternly tried.

It was a stern trial, also, to say good-by and go our separate ways to the opposite sides of the Andes once more. I had a long row to hoe on the Colorado language before I could think about Quichua, but I went back to San Miguel more determined than ever to do the job, to coach Doreen and Barbara in the use of the materials I had collected so that they could carry on by themselves, and then to move out and go to the eastern jungle where I could start on Quichua.

I wrote Katherine von Schlegel's hymn in my diary:

> Be still my soul: thy best, thy heavenly Friend
> Through thorny ways leads to a joyful end.

> Be still my soul: thy God doth undertake
> To guide the future as he has the past.
> Thy hope, thy confidence let nothing shake;
> All now mysterious shall be bright at last.

Shadow of the Almighty (Grand Rapids: Zondervan, 1970).

142

18

An Alphabet for *Tsahfihki*

The language work became a great deal harder without Macario's greatly needed help. There was no way to carry it on in any organized fashion. I went to the Indian houses from time to time and often found no one at home, for the women would be at their planting and the men out hunting. One day I had an hour with one of the shyest Colorado women. I had gone by muleback two hours to her house, and as we sat by the fire, I began to ask questions and write down words. She soon saw what I was about, and patiently repeated things so that in a short time I had forty-five words and phrases. These I took home and filed, some with meanings and some without, for future analysis. Every shred of data helped.

One day Samuel, the chief's brother, came to help me with the language, and I invited him in to lunch. When I complimented him on his good use of Spanish, he said the equivalent of "Well, lady, I get around. Remember I am acquainted with Guayaquil." (Guayaquil was the largest port city.) He was perfectly groomed and painted. Next time, he told me, he would come for the whole day—he would even spend a night if I wished, so as to give me plenty of time to "ask words."

Manuel, Soledad's son, had promised several times that he would give me "lessons" in his language. It seldom was convenient for him, however, and he would offer many excuses. One day he rode past my gate, his usually well-greased and reddened hair sticking out in all directions, his legs muddied. He waved his cigarette vaguely in the direction of town and called out, "Tomorrow, señorita! I am *ocupadísimo*!" and rode on.

Another man came one day when I had been begging God to send me someone, a man I hardly knew, painted, greased, combed, and heavily perfumed, and sat down with me on the porch. I asked him if he understood what it was that I wanted, and how much he would want to be paid. No need at all to pay him, he said, he would stop in whenever he could. My pronunciation, he said, was perfect, and he was sure I would soon be speaking like a real Colorado. When an hour was up and I thanked him, he said, "Don't you have more words to ask me? I can stay longer if you like." I had all the material I could handle for the moment—compiling all he had given me would take hours. I asked him to come back another time, which he affably promised to do.

Wistfully, I recalled the regular hours with Macario, the comparative ease with which I could learn the meaning of

Tsahfihki phrases through the medium of Spanish. This having to depend on chance encounters was a desultory method at best, and I was discouraged.

When, on a Sunday morning, two Colorado women came into the clearing to ask me if I would accompany them on a trip to Quito, I packed up at once. I would have a nine-hour truck ride in which to talk to them, then the opportunity to show them the city and hear their comments, and the ride home. It was an unparalleled language opportunity, but the plan came to nothing. They refused to sit with me on the banana truck (it had not occurred to me that to sit with me would be, in their eyes and in the eyes of the other passengers, a serious breach in propriety), and when we arrived in Quito, they decided, instead of spending the night with me, to return on the next shift to Santa Domingo. Whatever it was that had made them decide to come to Quito I never learned. They certainly accomplished nothing, and my own hopes of spending time with them dissolved.

It is hard for a young person with high ideals to learn that people cannot be hustled. They cannot be hustled into the kingdom of God, and it is well to remember Christ's own descriptions of that kingdom: leaven and seed, things that work slowly and out of sight. We long for visible evidence of our effectiveness, and when it is not forthcoming, we are tempted to conclude that our efforts never had anything to do with the kingdom. I was inclined to think such thoughts. Why didn't a regular informant turn up? What was the good of such a haphazard method of study? Why, when someone has given himself to missionary work, are results so meager? Was it worth our while to go on? I went on anyway, taking advantage of every possible opportunity to be in Colorado company.

Barbara and I walked one day to a house where an old man was said to be very sick. We found him, not lying on a bed in the house but wandering around outside, a walking skeleton. He seemed rational enough, but said that lying on the bed made him tired. Barbara persuaded him to lie down on some banana leaves so that she could give him an injection, but it was difficult to find a soft place for the needle. She gave quinine, assuming it was malaria, but the possibility of yellow fever did occur to us. A year or two before, forty-two Colorados had died of yellow fever, and the threat hung over us. The buzz of a mosquito could be not merely annoying but frightening. The old man's family was sure that he would soon die, but they looked on the coming of the señorita to give an injection as a normal part of the prelude to death, and they were glad we had come. They gave us a supper of mashed banana, boiled banana, and dried fish, and helped us to write down a few more words of their language. Then we lay down to sleep on a couple of balsa benches. At midnight when Barbara rose to give more medicine and switched on her "electric torch," we saw that the place was alive with cockroaches, huge ones. "Oh, I say!" she whispered, and turned off the torch so as not to have to look at them.

There was a day in April called the Saturday of Glory, a big fiesta day for the Colorados. When I asked what Saturday of Glory meant, they told me it was the Saturday of Glory, their big fiesta. "And what is the Saturday of Glory?" I asked. "It is a fiesta," and no one could explain it further.

The Colorados had long since forgotten their religion—
if they ever had one of their own. Most of them wore on
their painted chests the medals given them by the priest,
along with beads, safety pins, buttons, and mirrors strung
on palm fiber. Most of them had never been to a Mass but
had probably looked inside the huge wooden church in Santa
Domingo and seen the painted saints and frightful murals
showing what happens to bad Catholics or non-Catholics. If
they had any idea that the Saturday of Glory had anything to
do with the priest or the church, they kept it to themselves.
It was their own day, and they took over our clearing.

They began to arrive at midmorning, four little boys first
of all, who went straight to Barbara's house, where Vicente
was, and sat down in silence. They wore their short, black-
and-white striped skirts pulled tightly about the hips, fastened with a brightly colored cloth belt. Their hair was like
red patent leather, smoothly plastered with Vaseline and
achiote, hardly a single hair distinguishable from the rest.
Their faces and bodies were red, striped and polka-dotted
with black. What a lot of work they had gone to to produce
the effect! Over their shoulders they had slung new lengths of
bright cloth—orange, yellow, or aqua. On their wrists they
wore wide silver bracelets, their teeth and lips were blackened
with dye, and the house reeked with perfume bought from
the drugstore in town. By eleven o'clock the clearing was
swarming with red people, so brilliant a spectacle against
the green jungle backdrop with their black hair and the
wild, bold colors of their scarves, skirts, and ribbons (for
the women had ribbons of many colors fluttering in their
hair) that I had the feeling they had consented to put on this

147

performance for the benefit of us white people. It was they, really, who belonged to the forest—not we—and ordinarily they melted into it so they could not be found, but on this day out of the whole year they made their appearance extravagantly, as if to say, "Lo, here we are. Behold us now, for you will behold us no more unless we choose."

Our houses became theirs on that day. With or without invitation, they made themselves at home, streaming in through the doors, sitting on the floor or the furniture, whichever seemed the more comfortable, inspecting everything inside and out. We missionaries offered them cinnamon water while the others gave liquor. Most of the Indians had brought their own bottles of *chicha*, a drink derived from sugar cane pressed with a wooden press and left to ferment in huge balsa wood canoes made for that purpose. They passed the bottles from mouth to mouth, the greeting of the day being the exchange of bottles. Women who did not like *chicha* always accepted the bottle graciously, took a mouthful, and spat it on the floor. Babies were given a leaf soaked in *chicha* to suck on so that they would acquire the taste.

With the women had come, of course, all the babies and children, all the pets—monkeys, parrots, marmosets, and sloths. (Their dogs were left at home. A dog was not a pet to them. He was a servant, useful for hunting only if he was kept starved.) The floor of our house was soon awash with all the spitting and puddling, and strewn with banana peels and cigarette butts. I moved around with my notebook and pencil, getting words here and there, using the ones I had learned by now, trying to be friendly. There was a spirit of increasing camaraderie as the *chicha* and liquor had its effect, and the Indians, conscious for once that they were in charge, were no longer timid or obsequious but showed a largeness of heart toward us. We seemed harmless enough to them today, I suppose, and they could afford to humor us.

The chief, a man perhaps in his forties, with a genial face and a strapping build, not distinguishable from the others by his dress or his paint, came and sat on our porch and played his accordion. I had not met him before, but had heard of him as one of the most famous witch doctors in Ecuador. It was said that Indians and white people came from Colombia and Peru to be treated by him, and Doreen found that he could discuss anatomy almost as knowledgeably as doctors in England. He was most polite and cordial to me, and when he had played a few tunes and had a few drinks, he came and took my hand and began a long tale in a confidential murmur in my ear, about some of his relatives. I hardly got even the gist of it, since his Spanish deteriorated by the minute, and at last he lapsed into *Tsahfihki*, a little of which I could understand, and some of which I wrote down for future study.

Later in the afternoon, when nearly all the men were drunk, there was fighting and dancing and singing. Barbara, Doreen, and I were sitting in Barbara's house, talking with some Colorado women when the door burst open and in lunged one of the biggest of the Colorado men, waving a gun and whimpering.

"They want to fight me. They want to fight me and I am too small and weak. Save me!"

It appeared that somehow in the minds of the Indians, where we lived constituted a kind of sanctuary, a place where events that would make up the normal course of their lives would be suspended. Most of the time this would be a good reason for avoiding us. Sometimes, when an interruption was a thing to be desired, it was a reason for coming to us.

One Indian sidled up to me and suggested that I marry him. He was tired of his wife, he said, and it was time for a change.

Nearly a month went by after the fiesta during which no mail came from Jim because of avalanches on the road to Santo Domingo-Quito. There was no gasoline for our lamps either, and we were running out of candles and kerosene fast. Dorothy and Doreen were both in Quito and could not get back or send any word to us. At last those who were commissioned to repair the road got around to repairing it, and trucks began to move, our coworkers returned with mail and supplies, and my reading in the *Daily Light* was "I have seen, I have seen the affliction of my people which is in Egypt, and I have heard their groaning and am come down to deliver them." It is astonishing how easy it is to see oneself as in the bonds of Egypt's Israelite slaves, even if the bonds are nothing more than a few weeks' isolation and inconvenience. It is a merciful Lord indeed that sees that sort of "affliction" and hears those pusillanimous groans.

"There failed not ought of any good thing which the Lord had spoken unto the house of Israel. All came to pass . . . and it shall be said in that day, lo, this is our God, we have waited for him, and he will save us." So read the *Daily Light*. We were doing a lot of waiting, as always, in San Miguel, but I was waiting to get out of there and get to where I could study Quichua.

150

In May, Jim and I met in Quito again, and together rode a banana truck to Santo Domingo, horses to San Miguel, where he spent a few days. He preached in the Sunday meeting and made friends easily with our congregation. The women were extremely pleased to meet my *novio*. We had some pleasant evenings, sitting on the railing of our back porch together, watching an apricot moon float above the mystic trees of the *plaza* where the old white ox munched softly.

Dorothy's suitor visited her during this time and we said, "Be careful. Give him a chance to prove his conversion." She was satisfied that he had, and told him the next day she would marry him.

I rode back to Santo Domingo with Jim and watched him disappear up the road in a truck, feeling for what seemed the hundredth time the desolation of not knowing when I would see him again, not knowing what his plans were, or how high on his list our marriage might be.

It was a struggle to concentrate again on *Tsahfihki*, but I was close to making of the phonetic alphabet a phonemic one. This was my primary goal, and as I went along I was trying to explain the use of the material to Doreen and Barbara so that they could take it up where I left off.

A letter came from Jim several weeks after he left, saying that his bag had been stolen from the top of the truck. It had in it his good wool trousers, a new pair of boots, a pen and notebook containing our house plans, his beloved harmonica, a light meter and camera, and a box of the selected best slides he had ever taken. His letter sounded weary and depressed, and I felt the same as I read it. "They are only things," I told myself, "most of them things that money could buy. But the slides?" There was no way to replace the slides. Maybe God wanted me to let go not only of material possessions but of sentiment as well.

June 16 was the day when I finished the alphabet for *Tsahfihki*, or *Ȼafihki*, as I had decided to spell it in order to reduce the number of symbols. Instead of feeling triumphant, I was aware that the job had taken me longer than necessary, and I felt guilty for having allowed so many things to distract me. My labor "turned to dust," I wrote, and then I read the day's portion of *Daily Light*, which said ironically, "I have fought a good fight, I have finished my course, I have kept the faith." O Paul, O noble apostle, I feebly struggle, you in glory shine!

> And I thought then of a gospel song,
> Shall I empty-handed be
> when beside the crystal sea
> I shall stand before the everlasting throne?

19

The End of the Matter

A missionary family in the Oriente, or eastern jungle, invited me to come to their station to live while I began the study of Quichua. It was not hard to accept, and to leave the big, gloomy thatched house in San Miguel with its admixture of memories—the births, deaths, struggles, failures, losses, and all the days and weeks of common, ordinary missionary life when I accomplished nothing visible or tangible, when I often wasted time and wished I were elsewhere and allowed my thoughts to go off in all directions except where they belonged. Dorothy was engaged; Doreen, too, had made up her mind to marry Abdón; Barbara was making progress in the Colorado language and hoped to start a school for the Indians; and my language files and notebooks would provide a foundation for the future translation work that I felt sure someone would do, and I was glad to go.

Dos Rios was a Christian and Missionary Alliance station where a family named Conn had been working for some time. Nearby was the little frontier town of Tena in the province of Napo-Pastaza, named for two of the Amazon's headwaters. I went to Tena via a Missionary Aviation Fellowship plane and was met by Carol Conn and some Indians who carried my baggage and ferried us across the Mishahuallí River by dugout canoe. A long sandy trail bordered by orange trees and pasture led up to the white clapboard house on a hillside. Carol gave me the guest room, a large, light, pleasant room on the second floor with open screened windows looking across the pasture and river to the hills beyond Tena. Jim Elliot was beyond those hills.

I set to work at once on the study of Quichua. I went at it more fiercely than I had tackled either Spanish or *Tsahfihki*, for while these held out to me eternal rewards, the learning of Quichua held a clear-cut temporal one by which I am afraid I was more powerfully motivated.

I pestered the life out of Carol Conn, who spoke Quichua fluently, and any Indians who came by. I stood around in the kitchen with Lucrecia, a half-Indian, half-white girl who knew Spanish and Quichua equally well and could teach me and correct me while she cooked or washed dishes. I attended school and chapel services and Sunday meetings and Bible studies so that I could listen to the sound of the language, and because it is, it is said, one of the easiest languages in the world, it did not take me long to begin to understand.

It was only a few weeks after my arrival that I received a letter from Doreen, telling me that all of my Colorado language materials had been stolen. They had been in a suit-case that (and how many times had this happened during the past year?) disappeared from the top of a bus.

I sat at the big window and looked across the Mishahuallí River toward the hills, trying to absorb what the letter had said.

Everything I had done in nine months in San Miguel de los Colorados was undone at a stroke.

But no. It couldn't be. We would get it all back somehow. Lord, let it not be.

I read the letter again and again. The filebox, the note-books, the charts—all of it gone. All of it, of course, in my own handwriting. There were no copies of anything.

It was, after Maruja's and Macario's deaths, Lesson Three for me. Another experience of stripping. The tenth Psalm came to my mind: "Why dost thou hide thyself in times of trouble?" And, as before, I heard no reply to that and other questions. There was no light, no echo, no possible explana-tion. All the questions as to the validity of my calling, or, much more fundamental, God's interest in the Colorados' salvation, in any missionary work—Bible translation or any other kind—all these questions came again to the fore.

To be a follower of the Crucified means, sooner or later, a personal encounter with the cross. And the cross always entails loss. The great symbol of Christianity means sacri-fice and no one who calls himself a Christian can evade this stark fate. It is not by any means an easy thing to recognize, within a given instance of personal loss, the opportunity it affords for participation in Christ's own loss. What, we ask ourselves, can this possibly have to do with *that*? We are not by nature inclined to think spiritually. We are ready to assign almost any other explanation to the things that happen to us. There is a certain reticence to infer that our little troubles may actually be the vehicles to bring us to God. Most of us simply grin and bear them, knowing they are the lot of all human beings, and our memories being marvelously selective, we simply cancel them out, none the better for the lessons we might have learned.

Certainly I did not think immediately of the loss of my language notes as God's way of breaking through certain categories of mine. I was dumbfounded to realize that all that work was down the drain. I was also furious at whoever stole that suitcase and undoubtedly discarded that priceless paper. I suppose I wondered, too, whether the owner of the suitcase had perhaps been careless. But there was nothing to be done about it at all, no hope of recovery, and that was that.

But my first year as jungle missionary was not yet quite up, and Lesson Four was on its way.

One small responsibility that Carol delegated to me was that of standing by on the regular "morning contact." There was a shortwave radio network by which all the jungle mission stations communicated each morning with the Missionary Aviation Fellowship base. I was only too happy to be asked to do the calling in for Dos Rios—it meant that I might occasionally hear Jim's voice, "Shandia standing by." Once in a while there was even "traffic"—messages of a business nature—for me to pass on to him from Dos Rios.

One morning his voice came through the usual squeals and beeps and whistles with which we nearly always had to contend. He sounded agitated. I strained my ears. The entire station of Shandia—five buildings—had been demolished in a flood.

Jim had worked on that station all during the time I had worked on *Tsahfihki*. He had amassed five hundred hand-planed boards for future buildings. These presented five hundred man-days' work. He had repaired three old buildings and constructed two new ones. All of it now had gone down the Napo River. It was probably in the Amazon by the time I received his message.

"The voice of the Lord is upon the waters; the God of glory thundereth. . . . The Lord will give strength unto his people; the Lord will bless his people with peace."

It was only gradually during the months that followed that I saw that to God nothing is finally lost. All the scriptural metaphors about the death of the seed that falls into the ground, about losing one's life, about becoming the least in the kingdom, about the world's passing away—all these go on to something unspeakably better and more glorious. Loss and death are only the preludes to gain and life. It was a temptation to foreshorten the promises, to look for some prompt fulfillment of the loss-gain principle—maybe, for example, the suitcase would turn up and everybody would rejoice because prayer had been answered, because we had come through another lesson with flying colors, because we would have proof that God won't let His work be set back, that He does always and everywhere put a wall around His servants and their service for Him.

My mind boggled in trying to imagine how the Lord might undo the Shandia disaster. Lesson Four was in a class with

Lessons One and Two. Maruja and Macario were dead and buried. The mission station was demolished. Even the most sinewy faith in the world could not bring them back. But hope still survived for the suitcase. The Lord whose eyes run to and fro throughout the whole earth knew where that suitcase and its precious contents were. I prayed for its recovery. Surely, Lord . . . ?

The suitcase did not turn up.

And so it often is. Faith, prayer, and obedience are our requirements. We are not offered in exchange immunity and exemption from the world's woes. What we are offered has to do with another world altogether.

A story is told of Jesus and His disciples walking one day along a stony road. Jesus asked each of them to choose a stone to carry for Him. John, it is said, chose a large one while Peter chose the smaller. Jesus led them then to the top of a mountain and commanded that the stones be made bread. Each disciple, by this time tired and hungry, was allowed to eat the bread he held in his hand, but of course Peter's was not sufficient to satisfy his hunger. John gave him some of his.

Some time later Jesus again asked the disciples to pick up a stone to carry. This time Peter chose the largest of all. Taking them to a river, Jesus told them to cast the stones into the water. They did so, but looked at one another in bewilderment.

"For whom," asked Jesus, "did you carry the stone?"

Epilogue

That "school year" of 1952–53 was a momentous one indeed. I began to learn the deep meaning of the cross in the life of a believer. God was quietly and steadily teaching me what I now, somewhat ruefully, call the "four kindergarten lessons"—the deaths of Maruja and Macario, the loss of the year's language work, and the destruction of all Jim's buildings. They were to prepare me for yet more formidable courses.*

As we learn to know God, we learn that His ways are past finding out. We gaze into the abyss and cry "Why?" Seldom does the Lord of the Universe explain Himself in any terms other than those found in His holy Word. "The secret things belong to the LORD our God, but the things revealed belong to us and to our children forever, that we may follow all the words of this law" (Deut. 29:29).

*See *Through Gates of Splendor, The Savage My Kinsman, The Path of Loneliness, A Path Through Suffering.*

A hymn that we had sung in our family prayers at home held me steady through many a dark time to come.

> If thou but suffer God to guide thee and hope in
> Him through all thy ways
> He'll give thee strength whate'er betide thee and bear
> thee through the evil days;
> Who trust in God's unchanging love builds on a rock
> that naught can move.
> Obey, thou restless heart, be still, and wait in cheer-
> ful hope, content
> To take whate'er his gracious will, His all-discerning
> love, hath sent;
> Nor doubt our inmost wants are known to Him who
> chose us for His own.
>
> Sing, pray, and swerve not from his ways, but do
> thine own part faithfully.
> Trust His rich promises of grace, so shall they be ful-
> filled in thee.
> God never yet forsook in need the soul that trusted
> Him indeed.
>
> Georg Neumark

God makes no mistakes. He does not fall asleep. He does not forget His loved children. He asks us, every day, no matter what circumstances or adversities we find ourselves in, to *trust* and *obey*. He has so arranged things that we may not often fathom His sovereign purposes, but now and then He vouchsafes to us a glimpse of what He is up to.

Many years after my time in Ecuador, my husband and I sat at the dinner table of a pastor and his wife. She told us of the agonizing experience of going through a divorce. To my astonishment she said that this book, *These Strange Ashes*, had helped her through that ordeal. I could not imagine how my experience had any relation to hers.

The next day I spoke to a group in this lady's church, telling the story of that first year with the Colorados and the hard lessons assigned to me then. Later the pastor's wife asked me if God had ever revealed to me any part of His purpose in allowing those things to happen.

"Why, yes!" said I, "Last evening!"

She looked at me in puzzlement. "Last evening?"

"At your dinner table."

More puzzlement.

"You told me how the Lord had comforted you through the reading of that book. Might He have been thinking of you way back in 1953? Did He not carefully and lovingly arrange—for *you*—what were for me 'strange ashes'?"

A little light went on in her head. "Oh! Oh, *yes!*"

We should not be surprised at the mysterious ways in which our loving Father works all things together for good. We need to go back again and again to God's guidebook, the Bible. It's all spelled out for us there. For example, the apostle Paul wrote to the Corinthians, "Just as the sufferings of Christ flow over into our lives, so also through Christ our comfort overflows. If we are distressed, it is for your comfort and salvation; if *we* are comforted, it is for *your* comfort, which produces in you patient endurance . . ." (2 Cor. 1:5–6, emphasis mine).

The apostle Peter wrote, "Dear friends, do not be surprised at the painful trial you are suffering, as though something

strange were happening to you. But rejoice that you partici-
pate in the sufferings of Christ, so that you may be overjoyed
when his glory is revealed" (1 Pet. 4:12–13).

I think there is another little lesson for all of us here. Christ
is sufficient. We do not need "support groups" for each and
every separate tribulation. The most widely divergent sorrows may all be taken to the foot of the same old rugged
cross and find there cleansing, peace, and joy.

In 1995 my husband and I visited my dear old friend Doreen, now in her seventies, and her Ecuadorian husband,
Abdón Villarreal. They still faithfully work with the Colorados. Some have become earnest Christians and there is a
small church. The New Testament was translated into the
Colorado language by Bruce Moore and his wife, translators
with the Summer Institute of Linguistics.

DISCOVER

ELISABETH ELLIOT'S
MINISTRY, WRITING & TEACHING

Now all in one place at

ElisabethElliot.org

The Elisabeth Elliot Foundation was created based on the life, love, and ministry of Elisabeth and Jim Elliot. Through the ElisabethElliot.org website and other media platforms, the Foundation brings together the writings and ministries of the Elliot family in an evolving repository of their work, a resourceful collection of their writings and teachings, and a place to honor their legacy. It serves as an ongoing, worldwide outreach to help further the Foundation's mission to give

Hope in Suffering
Restoration in Conflict
Joy in Obedience to the Lord Jesus Christ